Elisa Marshall and Benjamin Sormonte opened maman to fill a void in their hearts. They wanted to create a warm, cozy place for people to come together and savor a freshly baked madeleine or slice of savory quiche with the comfort and familiarity of being in their own living room. This collection of 100 recipes spans bestselling dishes from their locations in New York City, Montreal, and Toronto—like Banana-Lavender Cornmeal Waffles with Vanilla Mascarpone, Cumin Chickpea Salad, and the Nutty Chocolate Chip Cookies made famous by none other than Oprah.

"The first time I walked into maman to grab a croissant for my kids, I was lovestruck by the charm and effortless elegance of the bakery. What drew me back to maman several times a week was the menu: a little fussy, a touch rustic, and just the right amount of sophistication that made eating the food feel like an act of self-love. This book is the perfect host gift but also one that will surely be earmarked, splashed with wine and chocolate from overuse, which in my mind is a smash."
    —Erin McKenna, owner
    of Erin McKenna's Bakery

"I'm such a big fan of maman's coffee shops. The food, the drinks, the décor, everything is so lovely and thought through. No surprise, Elisa and Benjamin's first cookbook is the same. Every page and recipe is so beautiful. It's as delightful to flip through as it is to cook from."
    —Kerry Diamond, founder
    of Cherry Bombe

"*Maman* is a stellar cookbook filled with mouthwatering and heartwarming recipes that, simply put, are food from the soul. Believe me when I tell you, this cookbook will forever have a space in your heart and in your kitchen."
    —Diala Canelo, author of
    Diala's Kitchen

"I am so happy to see Elisa and Ben's work in print. Their thoughtfulness in the creation of their products and spaces translates beautifully onto these pages. As a bakery owner myself, one always hopes that your children love your spaces the most. This is not the case with my son Isaac, who loves maman more than Gjusta. From one maman to another, I celebrate you."
    —Shelley Kleyn Armistead,
    CEO of Gjelina

"I am not just here for the blue-and-white china, although that alone would be enough!! Elisa and Ben's beautiful book is filled with delightful food, topped with artisanal charm. This favorite NYC breakfast spot is now accessible to every home cook!"
    —Laurel Gallucci, cofounder
    and CEO of Sweet Laurel

THE COOKBOOK

MAMAN

THE COOKBOOK

*all-day recipes
to warm your heart*

ELISA MARSHALL
AND BENJAMIN SORMONTE

WITH LAUREN SALKELD

CLARKSON POTTER/PUBLISHERS

NEW YORK

for Janice and Joelle,
who have given us so
many delicious memories

contents

a note from our mamans

I was very lucky to have my darling maman at home when my four siblings and I were growing up. My maman spent her days in the kitchen, which meant we always came home from school to an assortment of pies, cakes, and cookies. This practice instilled a great love for food and cooking in our entire family. And thankfully, maman taught me how to make all of these delicious treats, skills I would eventually pass on to my own family.

Because of my maman, baking and cooking became my passion. I studied at culinary school and spent years working as a private chef, but my greatest joy was always cooking for my husband and two daughters. As a young girl, Elisa found a place beside me in the kitchen, and I hoped her love for cooking and hosting would lead her to follow in my and my dear maman's footsteps. I am so proud she took her passion a step further and realized her dream to open her very own café.

The café was built with love. We spent several weeks together testing recipes, getting the space ready to open, and creating memories along the way. Elisa commissioned me to paint one-of-a-kind antique chairs and write calligraphy menus on wall-sized mirrors, among what seemed like a million other tasks. Initially, our work seemed endless, but it was an exciting project to be a part of, and our family was so happy to help bring Elisa and Ben's vision to life. We were, at long last, making a special place to realize the beautiful dream of a little girl, a place where our family recipes would be shared and enjoyed. And now, with this book, our café and bakery, maman, can be experienced by even more people. From my maman to me, to Elisa, to you.

Janice Marshall
ELISA'S MAMAN

From a very young age, I watched my great-grandmother cook for large groups and saw how much imagination she brought to creating meals, especially on the grill or in the terra-cotta dishware she'd made herself. I loved those long family meals and soon developed my own passion for making and sharing food, especially after a game of basketball, another passion of mine, and one I would eventually share with my son Benjamin.

When I became a maman, I was committed to feeding my two sons only the best and spent a lot of time in the kitchen, often helping them with their homework as I cooked. Soon my sons began baking cakes with me, and eventually they helped me cook everything else, too. Benjamin was always eager to learn and help, and he asked a ton of questions.

I am grateful I had this time with my sons and that I was able to impress upon them my passion for cooking. As they got older and left home, traveling and living abroad, they discovered new cultures and cuisines, which they combined with what I'd taught them, to create their own unique cooking styles and recipes. Now Benjamin brings his son, Yves, into the kitchen. I have no doubt they will cherish these experiences just as much as we did.

I am thankful to Benjamin and Elisa for creating maman as an homage to their mamans and families, and I continue to be impressed with the incredible dedication they've shown since opening their first location. I believe their customers' loyalty demonstrates how much they've learned in the kitchen and how hard they've worked to create such an extraordinary place.

Joelle Sormonte
BEN'S MAMAN

Lawrence Ferlinghetti
little boy
DOUBLEDAY
I'll See You in Paris
Michelle Gable
Thomas Dunne Books
The Cooking of Provincial France

what is maman?

Our customers motivate and inspire us to make maman better every day, and we are honored to be a part of their lives. These notes, written by a few regulars, describe what it's like to visit maman and how it really has become a home away from home for so many.

"It's a place to meet people from all over the world, who all come here for the same reason—to experience delicious things in a beautiful environment. Sharing a friendly exchange over good coffee and a warm cookie can start, end, or uplift anyone's day."

"A euphoric treat for the senses and the best of French-American cuisine and culture, curated to stimulate those with a rich appetite and lifestyle. From velvety espresso drinks to a perfectly seasonal lunch, enjoyed within an inspiring atmosphere— maman is perfect for a midday escape or to come together with family and friends."

"Maman is a gathering place, a place to feel special while still feeling at ease. And just as in any good maman's house, you can find comfort in the form of food, drink, or simply in sharing in the ambiance."

"Vintage, gorgeous, quaint…it's a home away from home in a city where most people do not feel at home. You're surrounded by beautiful yet familiar things that make you want to stay awhile and come back often."

"Maman embodies the kind of restaurant where you walk in and know your barista or waiter by their first name—everyone is always very friendly and accommodating, which is refreshing, being that it's not common in big cities."

"To me, maman is a little pocket of community in the middle of the bustling city, a beautiful spot that feels a little like home, perfect for celebrating birthdays and special occasions, gathering with a few friends, or enjoying a quiet coffee solo."

"Maman is solace from the 'big city.' It's like stepping into your childhood kitchen when times were simpler and cookies were sweeter."

"In a city of limitless options, I'm not a regular at many spots. It almost feels naïve to go back to the same coffee shop, the same restaurant, the same bakery, when there are consistently new places popping up that invite exploration. And yet I've found myself showing up at maman's door week after week. The lavender latte, the Tawni salad, the nutty chocolate chip cookie, the smell, the aesthetic are all timeless. They converge to create that unnameable ingredient that lifts your spirits, fosters connection, and, to be honest, feels a little magical."

introduction

ABOUT MAMAN:
A HOME AWAY FROM HOME

When you walk into any of our maman locations, the feeling is always the same. The aroma of culinary splendor wafts through the air, welcoming you inside, while the light buzz of conversation balances against the hiss of the espresso machine and the occasional clanging of pots. The exact details of each maman are unique, but features like exposed brick, rustic wood tables, mismatched china, and our signature blue-and-white patterns that are on everything from our to-go cups to our wallpaper create a familiar environment. The food always smells and tastes like something from your maman's kitchen, or maybe like a dish your grandmother taught you that you still make today. Coming into the café engages all your senses, embraces you, and makes you feel right at home.

Maman means "mother" in French, but for us, it also embodies the comforting, cozy feeling of home we wanted to create when we opened our first café in a former art gallery. At the time, late 2014, New York was filled with sleek spots that were all about being cool and trendy, but there weren't a lot of places to settle into with a good cup of coffee to concentrate on reading, writing, or sketching, or to lounge for a few hours enjoying a meal with friends, almost as if in your own living room. There also weren't spaces to gather around the table to celebrate all of life's special occasions, big or small.

We were both fortunate to grow up in families that loved to come together around food, and with mamans and grandmothers who were amazing cooks and bakers. We were far away from home and missing our families, with Elisa's in Canada and Ben's in France. We couldn't find exactly what we were looking for, so we decided to establish this sense of home for ourselves, which is how the café ultimately came to be. We set out to create a place that welcomes people with familiar sights, scents, and sounds—a place that feels like home.

We filled the space with furniture and décor inspired by our own childhood homes: a large wooden table surrounded by assorted vintage chairs, a china hutch, and vintage flatware. Even the bunnies that pop up in different forms at all our locations are drawn from the fact that we (like many others) both had beloved stuffed bunnies as children. We hoped these kinds of details would resonate with our guests, evoking thoughts of the past, stirring emotions, and helping instill that wonderful sense of home.

Of course, just as the kitchen is always the heart of the home, food was always going to be the heart of maman. When you open the door to any of our locations, you're drawn in by the inviting scent of something from the kitchen, be it cookies, quiche, or roast chicken—familiar aromas that evoke a bit of nostalgia.

As we were planning our menu, we kept returning to our families' recipes and traditions. It's even how we settled on the name maman, which conjures the feeling we wanted to create while also celebrating our mamans, both of whom ignited our passion for food and entertaining. By using the French word, we pay tribute to the French heritage and influences in our menu.

Years later, maman has multiple locations, along with a thriving catering and event business and a partnership with Paper Source that includes pop-up shops, stationery, and a party collection. Through the years and our expansion, we've stayed true to our original idea—to create a home away from home, a place where you can find comfort, along with delicious food, decadent desserts, and irresistible drinks.

Elisa grew up in Unionville, a quaint and picturesque suburb of Toronto—the perfect little town. Both her maman and grandmother loved to cook and bake, and from a young age, Elisa found herself similarly drawn to the kitchen. She spent hours by their sides, learning basics, like how to measure, but also discovering her own creative side. For her, it wasn't just about making food, it was also about how to serve it, which meant elaborately decorating cakes, creating special themed platters for holidays, and setting the long, sixteen-person wooden table that was handmade by Elisa's father (and that inspired the tables at maman).

After college, Elisa moved to Montreal to work in fashion marketing and public relations. That job led to event planning, which Elisa had a natural talent for and

that brought her back to her early love of entertaining. On the side, Elisa started wedding planning and freelance interior designing, and she even launched a cupcake catering company—all of which fed her creative side but also left her frustrated. She really wanted a job that brought her varied talents and creativity under one roof. Not long after that, she met Ben.

Six thousand miles away, in Montpellier, France, Ben grew up surrounded by food lovers. Weekends were about family, and the Sormontes spent Sundays in the kitchen and around the table. Ben's father is Italian, and his maman was born in Algeria, so the family's culinary inspirations have always been eclectic and international.

Like Elisa, Ben learned to cook and appreciate food from an early age, and

enjoyed leisurely meals with family and friends. He was also a talented basketball player with dreams of playing and studying in the United States, so when he was eighteen, he moved to Mobile, Alabama, with a scholarship to play NCAA Division 1 basketball at the University of South Alabama. Looking to further his education, Ben moved north to Montreal, where he found the perfect mix of North American and European sensibilities and studied law. After graduation, he took a job at a law firm working between Toronto and Montreal, where he met Elisa.

Mutual friends tried to set them up a number of times, but logistics and exes kept them apart. They ended up meeting by chance at a crowded bar, where Ben charmed Elisa with a story about being a famous French actor in town to film a movie. They chatted for a few minutes and exchanged numbers, but Ben's lie quickly caught up with him. Elisa couldn't find anything about this supposed actor online, but Ben found Elisa on Facebook and immediately realized she was the woman he had almost been set up with two years earlier. For their real first date, Ben took Elisa to dinner to apologize. That night, Elisa shared her dreams for what would become maman; Ben confessed that he, too, dreamed of opening a restaurant.

A few years later, those shared dreams became a reality. Together, we moved to Spain to run a restaurant and wedding venue in Ibiza, and then moved to New York City and worked side by side at a wine bar and a cocktail lounge. We were still dreaming of opening our own place someday when we discovered what could only be described as the perfect spot—an art gallery on Centre Street in Soho. With tin walls and ceilings, exposed brick, and original wood floors, it was rustic, charming, and cozy. It was everything we were looking for, and the gallery's lease was coming up. We immediately reached out to the landlord and realized that our dreams were about to come to life.

We had a bit of money saved and were lucky to have generous friends and family who helped us transform the space. Our parents came and chipped in, doing everything from sanding chairs to painting walls. Within a few months, we were ready to open maman. Although a chef was helping us, Elisa did a lot of the baking, ran the coffee operation and events, and handled branding and marketing, while Ben cooked a lot of the savory food, manned the counter, and managed the back end of the business.

We were overjoyed at the wonderful press maman received shortly after opening—soon, people were even driving from out of state to get our cookies! The atmosphere we had worked so hard to create was an instant hit with our guests, who started booking maman for showers, birthdays, and even weddings. We could barely keep up—and from there, business continued to take off.

We have since expanded with more locations in New York, as well as in other US cities and Canada—we've even launched pop-up cafés in Paris and St. Bart's. With each new café, we've been able to bring the maman experience to a new community, as well as grow our maman family. Now, we're even able to ship cookies coast to coast, bringing a little taste of maman to homes across the country.

ABOUT OUR BOOK:
MAMAN IN YOUR KITCHEN

Writing a cookbook has been a goal for almost as long as we've had maman. The café has been a way to share not only our recipes but also the comfort that comes from cooking and eating together. With this book, we're excited to bring that experience to an even larger community, including those who don't live near one of our locations. Our fans will be happy to finally have some of our most coveted recipes, but for us this book is more than just a collection of recipes. It's the next step in the maman journey, which is a love story at its core.

We opened maman as a couple, thrilled to build something together and work side by side, but our team quickly became our family. In addition to sharing their talents and creativity, they've also shared their own family recipes, which is why our menu—and now our cookbook—features recipes not just from our mamans and grandmothers, but also from our extended maman family. We wouldn't have it any other way.

While we work in the food industry, we're not professional chefs; we learned by doing. A few of the recipes in this book are a bit more challenging, but most are incredibly accessible, and all are written for home cooks. Our recipes are drawn from a repertoire of family classics that are both simple and adaptable, so you can cook and enjoy them time and time again. They are meant to draw you to the kitchen, inspire you to create, and then lead you to the table to nourish and connect with the ones you love.

We organized the book to reflect different ways you can enjoy the maman experience and our all-day café style. Part I is dedicated to breakfast and brunch and includes both sweet and savory options, while Part II features dishes that can be enjoyed throughout the day, from soups and salads to sandwiches and quiches. Part III is devoted to what maman is famous for, irresistible sweets, including cakes, cookies, and tarts, plus recipes and tips for making some of our delicious drinks at home.

We hope you'll think of this book as a scrapbook, a place where you can gather and record your ideas and inspirations. If you find a cake is too sweet, make a note to use less sugar next time. If you don't have cauliflower and discover broccoli works even better, write that down. Don't be afraid to scribble on the pages and jot down your ideas. When it comes time for you to pass these recipes on to your loved ones, you'll want them to know how you made them your own. With your special touches, this book will become a cherished heirloom for you and your family to treasure for years to come.

We've been delighted and honored by the response to maman, and with this book not only are we sharing some of our most beloved recipes, but we're also telling the stories behind them, all in the hope that you'll make them in your own kitchen. We wrote this book to help you enjoy the maman experience, whether that means hosting a brunch for your girlfriends, baking cookies for your kids, or treating yourself to our Lavender Hot Chocolate (page 237). Even more important, we hope our recipes and stories help you create new memories with your loved ones, both in the kitchen and around the table.

equipment

Antiquing is one of our favorite hobbies, and our house (especially our kitchen) is full of beautiful yet useful tools, gadgets, and entertaining pieces. We even have a motto that everything has to be attractive or functional; if an item doesn't fit one category or the other, it's out. If it fits both, we have to have it!

While we favor flea market finds, what's most important is that you have the tools you need and that you enjoy using them. In addition to basics like knives, cutting boards, baking sheets and sheet pans (the former are rimless; the latter have rims), bowls, a rolling pin, a whisk, and wooden spoons, these are our kitchen and entertaining essentials—plus a few nonessential but fun or helpful pieces we recommend.

ESSENTIALS

Measuring cups and spoons to measure dry ingredients and small amounts of liquid. Elisa's favorite tools are her grandmother's measuring set, which were passed down from her maman and bring back beautiful memories of them cooking together. If you're in the market for a new set, we recommend metal ones, connected by a ring so none of them gets lost.

Spouted glass measuring cups for measuring liquids. It's important to have one that lists both imperial and metric measurements. Our favorite is a 4-cup Pyrex model, because it's perfect for measuring, mixing, and pouring hot liquids.

Kitchen scale for weighing ingredients. This is a must-have for European recipes. A digital scale helps you easily convert between ounces and grams, but we also like pretty vintage versions, as they make for lovely kitchen décor.

Mini food processor for making pesto, sauces, spreads, and salad dressings. A full-size processor is also helpful, but we find a mini one handles most day-to-day jobs and is better for smaller quantities. Plus, it takes up less space and is easier to clean.

Electric mixer for all your baking needs. We're partial to the ease of a stand mixer, especially for powering through stiff doughs or anything that takes a while to whip or blend. However, many of our recipes, including most cookies and tarts, can easily be made with a handheld mixer, which also comes in handy for smaller jobs like whipping cream.

Waffle iron for homemade waffles—and our hash brown waffles (see page 60). You can go for a classic waffle iron, a Belgian waffle iron, or even a heart-shaped version, like the one Elisa has been using since childhood.

Cast-iron skillets for cooking sweet and savory recipes on the stove or in the oven. Invest in a large (12-inch / *30 cm*) skillet, as well as mini (6-inch / *15 cm*) ones for making smaller versions of our Provençal Eggs Ratatouille (page 58).

Tart pans for tarts and quiches. We recommend having one large (9½-inch / *24 cm*) pan, preferably with a removable base and scalloped edges, and six small (4-inch / *10 cm*) pans for making tartlets. For variety, we also like to bake tarts in a 14 × 5-inch (*35 × 12.5 cm*) rectangular pan. We prefer heavy-gauge tinned steel pans to ensure even baking.

Baking pans for sweet and savory treats. We prefer carbon steel pans, which are durable and heat evenly. For our naked cakes, we use either three small (6-inch / *15 cm*) or three large (9-inch / *23 cm*) round cake pans. For brownies and bars, we use a small (8- to 9-inch / *20 to 23 cm*) square baking pan or a 9 × 13-inch (*23 × 33 cm*) baking pan. We use Bundt pans to dress up simple cakes like our Pain D'Épices (page 37). Nonstick versions are super easy to use, but you can also grease a regular Bundt pan—look for unique ones in vintage shops or your grandmother's kitchen. For sweet and savory loaves, we use a 9 × 5-inch (*23 × 12.5 cm*) nonstick loaf pan, so the loaves pop right out and can be quickly drizzled with glaze. We use a 9½-inch (*24 cm*) springform pan for our Mandarin Orange Chocolate Cheesecake (page 178) as well as deep-dish pizzas and ice cream cakes.

Pastry mat or board for measuring the diameter as you roll out pie dough into rounds. We have a glass version, but silicone mats are also available. Look for one with both inch and centimeter measurements.

Cookie cutters to put a whimsical spin on cookies. We love to search antique markets for vintage versions, especially in France, as they can be used for almost any cookie that's rolled out, including Grandma Gracie's Shortbread Cookies (page 154) and Crumpet's Dog Cookies (page 166).

Wire racks for cooling. Racks let air circulate around baked goods, so they cool more quickly and evenly. We also place racks inside sheet pans for glazing cakes like our Pistachio Loaf Cake (page 171).

Ramekins for baking individual desserts. We use ½-cup (4 fluid ounce / *120 ml*) versions for Ben's Brûlée (page 222), but ramekins are also great for cheese platters or for serving hummus or other dips, and they are perfect for doing your mise en place before you start cooking or baking.

Spurtle for everyday kitchen tasks, including sautéing veggies, scrambling eggs, and scraping down the sides of a bowl. This versatile tool combines a wooden spoon and a spatula and is hands-down our favorite kitchen item. We love the cherrywood version from Mad Hungry.

Offset spatulas for spreading glazes and frosting cakes. These handy tools come in different sizes and are incredibly helpful for finishing cakes, especially naked-style cakes like our White Chocolate, Blueberry, and Lavender Naked Cake (page 181).

Piping bags and pastry tips for frosting and decorating cakes. These simple tools are endlessly useful—we use them to fill beignets and sandwich cookies, and when we want to create a nicer presentation for things like yogurt or avocado—so we always keep a roll of disposable plastic piping bags and a set of pastry tips on hand.

Wooden boards for serving. We use boards in various shapes and sizes for cheese platters and serving everything from sandwiches to cookies to quiche.

NOT-SO-ESSENTIALS

Kitchen conversion chart for quick and easy reference, so you don't have to stop and look up conversions when cooking. Ours is on a fridge magnet and we use it all the time!

Sticky notes for flagging recipes and making notes. If you look at our cookbook collection, you'll see tons of notes on the recipes we want to try, as well as changes we've made and even grocery lists.

To-go boxes and bags for leftovers. We cook, bake, and entertain *a lot,* and sharing with friends and family is one of the best parts of all that cooking and baking, so we always have boxes and bags handy to send our guests off with extras or to bring neighbors or coworkers a treat.

Wine opener because everyone knows you always cook better with a glass in hand.

crêpes with mushrooms
(page 53)

PART I

Sunrise

banana-lavender waffles
(page 28)

crème fraîche pancakes
(page 31)

toasted quinoa fruit salad
(page 47)

smoked salmon bowl
(page 60)

sweet beginnings

"I cook and bake with my kids all the time. Yes, it's messy, and yes, it takes longer, but I want them to have fond memories of our time together in the kitchen. I want them to think of cooking as fun and to associate mealtime with conversation, laughter, and connection. Cooking is my love language, and I hope that by cooking with and for my kids that they feel very loved."

—ANNA WATSON CARL,
chef and author, *The Yellow Table*

BANANA-LAVENDER CORNMEAL WAFFLES
WITH VANILLA MASCARPONE

serves 8

One of the best Christmas gifts Elisa ever received was a heart-shaped waffle iron. As she learned to cook, she used it often for her family's brunches—and it remains one of her favorite kitchen appliances today. We've added bananas and cornmeal to our recipe, which give the waffles a warm golden glow, a moist and fluffy center, and a lovely crisp crust. A touch of lavender reminds us of the South of France, where Ben grew up. You can use vanilla extract, but we love to splurge on vanilla beans, which add pretty black specks.

4 bananas (about 14 ounces / *400 g*), unpeeled

VANILLA MASCARPONE

1⅓ cups (*320 g*) mascarpone

⅓ cup (*75 ml*) maple syrup

½ teaspoon fine sea salt

½ vanilla bean, split lengthwise, or 1 tablespoon pure vanilla extract

WAFFLES

4 cups (*580 g*) all-purpose flour

2 cups (*330 g*) cornmeal

¾ cup (*128 g*) packed light brown sugar

2 tablespoons baking powder

1 teaspoon dried lavender powder (see Tip, page 189)

1 teaspoon fine sea salt

½ teaspoon ground cinnamon

4 cups (*960 ml*) whole milk

1 vanilla bean, split lengthwise, or 2 tablespoons pure vanilla extract

4 large eggs

⅓ cup (*75 ml*) sunflower oil

Vegetable oil spray

1. Preheat the oven to 350°F (*180°C*).

2. Arrange the unpeeled bananas in a single layer on a sheet pan and bake until blackened and beginning to ooze, about 20 minutes. Let cool to room temperature, about 20 minutes. Leave the oven on, but reduce the temperature to 200°F (*100°C*) to keep the waffles warm.

3. **MEANWHILE, MAKE THE VANILLA MASCARPONE:** In a stand mixer fitted with the whisk attachment, combine the mascarpone, maple syrup, and salt. Scrape in the vanilla seeds (or add the vanilla extract) and whip on high until smooth and sticking to the sides of the bowl, about 1 minute. Scrape down the sides of the bowl, then turn the mixer to medium-high and slowly add 2 tablespoons water, whisking just to incorporate. Scrape down the sides of the bowl again, then whip on high until fluffy, about 30 seconds. Be careful not to overwhip the mascarpone. Transfer to an airtight container and refrigerate until ready to use or for up to 4 days.

4. **MAKE THE WAFFLES:** When the bananas have cooled, heat a waffle iron according to the manufacturer's instructions.

5. In a medium bowl, stir together the flour, cornmeal, brown sugar, baking powder, dried lavender powder, salt, and cinnamon.

6. Pour the milk into the bowl of a stand mixer fitted with the whisk attachment. Scrape in the vanilla seeds (or add the vanilla extract). With the mixer running on low, add the eggs, 1 at a time, scraping down the sides of the bowl after each addition, and beat until fully incorporated. Peel the cooled bananas, add them to the bowl, and beat

RECIPE AND INGREDIENTS CONTINUE

3 or 4 bananas, sliced

Maple syrup, warmed

**Dried lavender flowers
(see Tip, page 189)**

**Toasted unsalted chopped
walnuts**

TIP: *Store waffles well
wrapped and frozen for up
to 2 months. Reheat (without
thawing) in a 450°F (230°C)
oven for 5 minutes.*

on medium until mostly broken up but still a bit
chunky, about 1 minute. With the mixer running on
low, gradually add the flour mixture in 4 additions,
then whip on medium speed until just combined,
about 30 seconds. With the mixer on medium,
gradually add the sunflower oil and whip for about
30 seconds to combine. A few lumps may remain in
the batter.

7. Coat the hot waffle iron generously with vegetable
oil spray. Using a ladle or measuring cup, scoop
2 cups (*480 ml*) of batter into the waffle iron,
spreading it to cover the entire surface. Close the
iron and cook until the waffle is light golden brown,
about 5 minutes. Keep the waffles warm in the oven
while you continue cooking.

8. Using a large spoon, spread a dollop of vanilla
mascarpone on each waffle. If desired, garnish with
banana slices, warm maple syrup, dried lavender
flowers, and walnuts, and enjoy immediately.

notes

_____

_____

_____

_____

_____

_____

CRÈME FRAÎCHE PANCAKES

WITH LEMON-BASIL COULIS
AND PECAN-PRETZEL CRUMBLE

serves 4

These unique pancakes were created by our former head chef Tawni Benick, and she considers this one of her best recipes. Crème fraîche makes the pancakes incredibly light and fluffy, while also lending richness and tanginess. You could go the traditional route and serve these pancakes with maple syrup, but the coulis and crumble combo makes for a truly unexpected sweet and salty topping. It's best to make the coulis the night before, so it has time to fully set in the fridge.

LEMON-BASIL COULIS

½ cup (*100 g*) granulated sugar

2 tablespoons cornstarch

2 tablespoons unsalted butter, cubed

2 tablespoons fresh lemon juice

⅛ teaspoon fine sea salt

1 cup (*30 g*) packed fresh basil leaves

½ cup (*20 g*) packed baby kale leaves

PECAN-PRETZEL CRUMBLE

¾ cup (*109 g*) all-purpose flour

⅓ cup (*20 g*) hand-crushed salted pretzels

⅓ cup (*40 g*) chopped raw unsalted pecans

¼ cup (*45 g*) packed light brown sugar

1 stick (4 ounces / *113 g*) unsalted butter, melted

1. **MAKE THE LEMON-BASIL COULIS:** In a medium saucepan, combine the granulated sugar and 1 cup (*240 ml*) water and heat over high heat, stirring until the sugar is completely dissolved, about 1 minute. Whisk in the cornstarch and bring to a boil. Remove the pan from the heat and continue whisking until the mixture stops bubbling. Add the butter, lemon juice, and salt and whisk until the butter is fully melted. Let cool to room temperature, about 30 minutes.

2. In a blender, combine half the sugar syrup with the basil and kale and blend on medium-high until the leaves are well chopped, about 30 seconds. Add the remaining sugar syrup and blend on medium-high until the mixture is bright green with only a few solid bits of basil and kale still visible, about 1 minute more. Transfer to an airtight container and refrigerate for at least 1 hour or preferably overnight. The coulis will thicken in the refrigerator.

3. **MEANWHILE, MAKE THE PECAN-PRETZEL CRUMBLE:** Preheat the oven to 350°F (*180°C*). Line a sheet pan with parchment paper.

4. In a medium bowl, whisk together the flour, pretzels, pecans, and brown sugar. Add the melted butter and mix with a rubber spatula until a wet dough forms. Spread the mixture in a thin, even layer on the prepared sheet pan—it may be easiest to use your hands—and bake until just starting to brown, about 10 minutes. Stir to break the mixture into crumbles, then bake until golden brown,

RECIPE AND INGREDIENTS CONTINUE

3 to 5 minutes more. Let the crumble cool on the sheet pan.

5. MAKE THE PANCAKES: Set the oven to 200°F (*100°C*) to keep the pancakes warm.

6. In a large bowl, whisk together the flour, granulated sugar, baking powder, and salt.

7. In a medium bowl, whisk together the crème fraîche and milk. Whisk in the eggs, followed by ⅓ cup (*75 ml*) sunflower oil.

8. Create a well in the center of the flour mixture. Add the crème fraîche mixture to the well and whisk the batter together, scraping down the sides of the bowl to incorporate all of the flour mixture. The batter will be very thick.

9. Heat 1 tablespoon sunflower oil in a large nonstick skillet over medium heat. When the oil is shimmering, reduce the heat to medium-low. Using a ladle or measuring cup, scoop about ½ cup (*120 ml*) of the batter into the skillet, then spread out the batter so the pancake is about 6 inches (*15 cm*) in diameter. Cook until the bottom is golden brown and just a few bubbles appear on top, 1½ to 2 minutes, then flip the pancake and cook until golden brown all over, 1½ minutes more. Keep the pancakes warm in the oven while you continue cooking, adding more oil to the pan as needed.

10. Stack the pancakes, dividing them among four plates. Top each with some lemon-basil coulis and sprinkle with pecan-pretzel crumble. Garnish with basil leaves and flowers, if desired, and serve.

PANCAKES

2½ cups (*363 g*) all-purpose flour

⅓ cup (*68 g*) granulated sugar

2½ teaspoons baking powder

1½ teaspoons fine sea salt

11½ ounces (*322 g*) crème fraîche

1⅓ cups (*315 ml*) whole milk

2 large eggs, lightly whisked

⅓ cup (*75 ml*) sunflower oil, plus more for cooking

Fresh basil leaves and flowers, for garnish (optional)

TIP: *Several components of this recipe can be made ahead. Store the coulis refrigerated in an airtight container for up to 5 days. Store the crumble at room temperature in an airtight container for up to 5 days.*

notes

CROISSANT PAIN PERDU

serves 8

....

Whenever we're in France visiting Ben's parents, the house is always full, as they love to host family and friends, especially for Sunday brunch. Pain perdu literally means "lost bread"; it's the original French toast. Our spin is made with day-old croissants, which we always seem to have around. The real beauty of this recipe is that it's prepped the night before, so you can sleep in and still enjoy a special brunch. To add a little Canadian flavor, we serve ours with maple syrup from the Montreal area. If you want something slightly sweeter and more indulgent, use pains au chocolat instead of croissants.

Vegetable oil spray

8 large day-old croissants (about 1¼ pounds / *560 g*), cut crosswise into 3 pieces

2 cups (*480 ml*) heavy cream

2 cups (*480 ml*) whole milk

¼ cup (*60 ml*) brandy, such as St-Rémy Cognac

1 tablespoon plus 1 teaspoon pure vanilla extract

8 large eggs

⅔ cup (*136 g*) sugar

Maple syrup, warmed, for serving

1. Coat a 9 × 13-inch (*23 × 33 cm*) baking dish with vegetable oil spray.

2. Arrange the croissants cut-sides down snugly in the baking dish, alternating the middle and end pieces and placing them at angles as needed to fit.

3. In a large liquid measuring cup, whisk together the heavy cream, milk, brandy, and vanilla. In a large bowl, beat the eggs. Add the sugar and whisk until fully incorporated. Add the cream mixture to the egg mixture in three additions, whisking until fully combined after each addition. Pour the mixture over the croissants, gently pressing down to be sure they are completely submerged. Wrap the pain perdu tightly with plastic wrap and refrigerate for at least 8 hours or overnight.

4. Preheat the oven to 350°F (*180°C*).

5. Bake the pain perdu, straight from the refrigerator, until the custard is firm and the center is set, about 45 minutes. Let cool for 10 minutes, then cut and scoop onto plates. Serve with warm maple syrup.

TIP: *Croissant pain perdu is best enjoyed immediately, but once baked, it can be refrigerated overnight and reheated in a 350°F (180°C) oven for about 15 minutes.*

notes

PAIN D'ÉPICES

makes one 9 1/2-inch (24 cm) bundt cake

There's a common stereotype that French bakers turn up their noses at Americans' overuse of spices, but pain d'épices proves otherwise. A classic French spice cake made with honey, molasses, cinnamon, cloves, ginger, and nutmeg, it has much in common with American gingerbread and demonstrates a shared appreciation for bold flavor. Bundt cakes remind Ben of his grandmother and are an easy way to turn a simple cake into something more special—look for unique pans in vintage shops or your grandmother's kitchen. Be sure to grease the pan all over—don't forget the center tube—to prevent sticking. We love to serve this cake slightly warm with a generous pat of butter, but it's also delicious at room temperature. Either way, it demands to be enjoyed with a good cup of coffee.

Vegetable oil spray

1½ cups (*360 ml*) whole milk

½ cup (*120 ml*) honey

½ cup (*120 ml*) molasses

3½ cups (*508 g*) all-purpose flour

3 tablespoons baking powder

2 teaspoons ground cinnamon

2 teaspoons ground cloves

2 teaspoons ground ginger

2 teaspoons grated nutmeg

3 large eggs

1½ cups (*300 g*) granulated sugar

Confectioners' sugar

1. Set a rack in the center of the oven and preheat to 325°F (*163°C*). Coat a 9½-inch (*24 cm*) fluted Bundt pan with vegetable oil spray.

2. In a small saucepan, combine the milk, honey, and molasses and bring to a simmer over medium heat.

3. In a medium bowl, whisk together the flour, baking powder, cinnamon, cloves, ginger, and nutmeg.

4. In a large bowl, whisk together the eggs and granulated sugar until fully combined. When the milk mixture is simmering, remove the pan from the heat and, while whisking vigorously, gradually add ¼ cup (*60 ml*) to the egg mixture. Repeat with another ¼ cup, then slowly add the remaining hot milk, whisking vigorously so the eggs don't scramble. Add half of the flour mixture and whisk just until there are no lumps, then add the rest of the flour mixture, whisking again just until there are no lumps.

5. Pour the batter into the prepared pan and bake until a toothpick inserted into the center of the cake comes out clean, about 1 hour.

6. Let cool for 15 minutes in the pan, then invert the cake onto a wire rack and let cool completely, about 1 hour. Dust with confectioners' sugar and serve.

TIPS:
Use a high-quality honey to bring out the flavor of this cake—we love to use a lavender honey.

Store at room temperature tightly wrapped in plastic wrap for up to 3 days.

notes

OLIVE OIL–BLOOD ORANGE LOAF

makes one 9×5-inch (23×12.5 cm) loaf

....

In the yard of Ben's childhood home stands a beautiful olive tree. When he was young, Ben and his brother collected buckets of olives from it to press at a local mill. Though continually disappointed with how little oil they produced, they remained motivated to collect more—they liked to see how the flavor differed depending on when the olives were harvested. Bright blood oranges pair perfectly with the richness of any high-quality olive oil, and their intense color makes for a particularly attractive loaf, but you can use regular oranges, lemons, or grapefruit. While we love this loaf for breakfast, with the addition of a simple glaze it can certainly double as dessert. For extra crunch, fold in a large handful of poppy seeds.

Vegetable oil spray and flour, for the pan

2 cups (290 g) all-purpose flour

1½ cups (300 g) granulated sugar

1½ teaspoons fine sea salt

½ teaspoon baking powder

½ teaspoon baking soda

3 blood oranges

1¼ cups (300 ml) extra-virgin olive oil

1¼ cups (300 ml) whole milk

3 large eggs

¼ cup (60 ml) orange-flavored liqueur, such as Grand Marnier

Confectioners' sugar, for garnish

notes

1. Set a rack in the center of the oven and preheat to 350°F (180°C). Coat a 9 × 5-inch (23 × 12.5 cm) loaf pan with vegetable oil spray and dust with flour. Set a wire rack inside a sheet pan.

2. In a medium bowl, whisk together the flour, granulated sugar, salt, baking powder, and baking soda.

3. Set aside 1 orange for garnish. Grate the zest of 1 of the remaining oranges, then juice both oranges and strain the liquid to remove any pulp. Measure out ¼ cup (60 ml) of the orange juice and reserve any extra for another use.

4. In a stand mixer fitted with the whisk attachment, combine the orange zest and juice with the olive oil, milk, eggs, and liqueur and whip until just combined. Add the flour mixture in 3 additions and mix on low, scraping down the sides of the bowl as needed, until fully incorporated, about 3 minutes total.

5. Pour the batter into the prepared pan and bake until a toothpick inserted into the center of the loaf comes out clean, 45 minutes to 1 hour.

6. Set the loaf pan on the wire rack and let cool for about 20 minutes, then invert the loaf onto the rack. Flip it again so the loaf is right-side up and let cool slightly. Dust with confectioners' sugar, then cut the reserved orange into thin slices, arrange on top of the loaf, and serve.

TIP: *Store the loaf in the refrigerator tightly wrapped in plastic wrap for up to 3 days.*

CHERRY-ROSEMARY CRUMBLE

serves 10

....

We served this sweet and savory crumble at the 2019 *Cherry Bombe* Jubilee, one of our favorite annual food events. While not a common pairing, we think woodsy rosemary and tart cherries complement each other perfectly. To get a jump on prep, you can assemble the crumble in a freezer-safe baking dish, wrap it in plastic wrap, and freeze for up to 1 week, then let it thaw while you preheat the oven and bake as directed. You can also make this crumble with sour cherries—just be sure to add an additional ½ cup (*100 g*) sugar to the filling. Neither version is super sweet, but this crumble also makes a fantastic dessert, especially if you top it with a scoop of vanilla ice cream.

CHERRY FILLING

9 cups (*1.2 kg*) fresh or frozen pitted sweet cherries

½ cup (*100 g*) granulated sugar

½ cup (*15 g*) packed fresh rosemary needles, chopped

¼ cup (*36 g*) all-purpose flour

2 teaspoons pure vanilla extract

1 teaspoon ground cinnamon

1 teaspoon fine sea salt

CRUMBLE TOPPING

2 cups (*290 g*) all-purpose flour

1½ cups (*140 g*) old-fashioned oats

¾ cup (*128 g*) packed light brown sugar

2 sticks (8 ounces / *225 g*) unsalted butter, cubed, softened

Fresh rosemary sprigs, for garnish (optional)

1. Preheat the oven to 400°F (*200°C*). Set a 9 × 13-inch (*23 × 33 cm*) baking dish on a sheet pan.

2. MAKE THE CHERRY FILLING: In a large bowl, combine the cherries, granulated sugar, rosemary, flour, vanilla, cinnamon, and salt and stir until the cherries are thoroughly coated.

3. MAKE THE CRUMBLE TOPPING: In a medium bowl, combine the flour, oats, and brown sugar. Add the softened butter and use your hands to incorporate it into the flour mixture until there is no visible flour or butter and the mixture has a crumbly, dough-like texture.

4. Spread the cherry filling evenly in the baking dish. Top with the crumble mixture, patting it down to create an even layer—the cherry filling will be visible between and under the crumble.

5. Bake until the crumble topping is golden brown and the cherry filling is bubbling, about 40 minutes. Let stand for 5 to 10 minutes, then garnish with sprigs of fresh rosemary (if using) and serve.

notes

....
....
....
....
....
....

ALMOND BUTTER–BANANA SPLIT PARFAITS

makes 2 parfaits

....

As wonderful as it is to indulge at breakfast, it's important to include healthier options, a lesson Elisa learned from her maman. When she was growing up, granola was a pantry staple, and she still loves how a homemade batch fills the house with its irresistible aroma. This recipe makes more than enough for the two parfaits. It is great to have on hand for breakfasts and snacks throughout the week. These banana split–inspired parfaits help make a healthier meal a bit more enticing for kids, but you can also simply layer the ingredients in bowls.

GRANOLA

6 cups (560 g) old-fashioned oats

2 cups (170 g) unsweetened shredded coconut

¾ cup (90 g) chopped raw unsalted pecans

¾ cup (102 g) raw unsalted pumpkin seeds

½ cup (55 g) sliced raw unsalted almonds

2 tablespoons ground cinnamon

2½ teaspoons ground ginger

1½ teaspoons fine sea salt

¾ teaspoon grated nutmeg

⅔ cup (158 g) almond butter

⅔ cup (150 ml) sunflower oil

½ cup (120 ml) maple syrup

¾ teaspoon pure vanilla extract

PARFAITS

1½ cups (360 g) plain Greek yogurt

2 bananas, halved lengthwise

1 (6-ounce / 170 g) container fresh berries, halved, or other seasonal fruit

Fresh mint leaves, for garnish (optional)

Honey, for drizzling

notes

....
....
....

1. **MAKE THE GRANOLA:** Preheat the oven to 300°F (150°C). Line two sheets pans with parchment paper.

2. In a large bowl, stir together the oats, coconut, pecans, pumpkin seeds, almonds, cinnamon, ginger, salt, and nutmeg.

3. In a medium bowl, combine the almond butter, sunflower oil, maple syrup, and vanilla and whisk until the ingredients are fully incorporated. Add to the oat mixture and using your hands, squeeze everything together to mix thoroughly until the oats are fully coated.

4. Spread the granola mixture in an even layer on the prepared sheet pans and bake for 12 minutes. Stir to break up the granola into crumbles, then bake until evenly golden brown, about 3 minutes more. Stir the granola again, then let cool completely on the sheet pans.

5. **MAKE THE PARFAITS:** Transfer the yogurt to a piping bag fitted with a medium round pastry tip. (Alternatively, spoon the yogurt into a resealable plastic bag and snip off the bottom corner.) Pipe 3 large balls of yogurt into the bottom of two banana split dishes. Tuck a banana half, cut-side facing in, into the yogurt on each side of both dishes. Arrange most but not all of the berries cut-side down on top of the yogurt. Sprinkle about ½ cup (60 g) granola over each parfait, then garnish with the rest of the berries and the mint (if using), drizzle with honey, and serve.

TIP: *Store the granola at room temperature in an airtight container for up to 2 weeks.*

BRANDY BRIOCHE FRENCH TOAST
WITH ESPRESSO MASCARPONE

serves 4

....

Inspired by the French toast Elisa's maman makes, this adults-only version features brandy and espresso, but you can omit them to make it kid-friendly. Brioche is a bread enriched with butter and eggs that has a very soft, fine crumb and an almost flaky exterior, so this French toast stays custardy on the inside yet crisps on the outside. You can make your own brioche (see page 199) or simply pick up a loaf from your favorite bakery. If you can only find it thinly sliced, stack the slices—they'll meld together. You need at least 6 hours to let the French toast set, so it's the perfect make-ahead dish for entertaining.

FRENCH TOAST

8 large eggs

2 cups (*480 ml*) whole milk

1 cup (*240 ml*) heavy cream

¾ cup (*150 g*) sugar

¼ cup (*60 ml*) brandy, such as St-Rémy Cognac

2 tablespoons pure vanilla extract

1 large unsliced loaf day-old brioche (about 1 pound / *450 g*)

ESPRESSO MASCARPONE

2½ cups (*600 g*) mascarpone

2 tablespoons maple syrup

¼ teaspoon fine sea salt

¼ cup (*15 g*) instant espresso powder

1 tablespoon warm water

3 tablespoons sunflower oil

SERVING

2 bananas, sliced (optional)

Finely ground coffee (optional)

Maple syrup, warmed

notes

1. **MAKE THE FRENCH TOAST:** In a large bowl, beat the eggs. Add the milk, heavy cream, sugar, brandy, and vanilla and whisk until fully combined. Spread a thin coat of the mixture on the bottom of a 9 × 13-inch (*23 × 33 cm*) baking dish.

2. Slice off the ends of the brioche (reserve for another use), then cut the loaf crosswise into slices roughly 2 inches (*5 cm*) thick—you should have 5 or 6 slices. Dip each slice into the batter, turning to coat fully, then arrange snugly, side by side, in the baking dish. Pour any remaining batter over the brioche. Tightly cover the baking dish with plastic wrap and refrigerate for at least 6 hours or overnight.

3. **MAKE THE ESPRESSO MASCARPONE:** In a medium bowl, combine the mascarpone, maple syrup, and salt and whisk until fully combined.

4. In a small bowl, whisk the instant espresso powder with the warm water until fully dissolved. Add to the mascarpone mixture and whisk until fully combined and an even, light-tan color. Refrigerate until ready to use.

5. About 1 hour before serving, remove the French toast from the refrigerator and let it come to room temperature. Set the oven to 200°F (*100°C*) to keep the French toast warm.

6. Heat 1 tablespoon of the sunflower oil in a large nonstick skillet over medium heat. When the oil is shimmering, reduce the heat to medium-low and add 2 slices of brioche. Place a heavy saucepan directly on top of the brioche to press it into the skillet. Cook until golden brown on the bottom, about 6 minutes, then flip over the slices and cook the other side the same way until golden brown all

over, 6 minutes more. Keep the French toast warm in the oven while you continue cooking, using 1 tablespoon of sunflower oil for each batch.

7. **TO SERVE**: Arrange each slice of French toast on a plate and generously dollop with the espresso mascarpone. If desired, sprinkle with banana slices and finely ground coffee. Serve with warm maple syrup.

TIPS:

In lieu of instant espresso powder, you can use regular instant coffee, preferably a dark roast, but you'll need to add a little extra to approximate the rich, roasted flavor of espresso.

Store the espresso mascarpone refrigerated in an airtight container for up to 5 days.

TOASTED QUINOA FRUIT SALAD

serves 4

....

Ben created this recipe as a way to transform a light dish into a well-balanced breakfast. Fresh mint and basil are a great complement to the sweetness of the fruit, while the quinoa adds toasty notes and a bit of crunch, as well as protein and fiber. When entertaining, we serve this colorful salad in a teacup and saucer, which is a fun presentation and easy to do at home. This is our usual spring and summer version, while for fall and winter, we use apples, pears, pomegranates, grapes, and figs.

1 small seedless watermelon (about 4 pounds / *1.8 kg*)

½ small pineapple (about 1 pound 5 ounces / *600 g*)

¼ cup (*45 g*) red quinoa

2 cups (*305 g*) blueberries

2 cups (*340 g*) blackberries

1 cup (*170 g*) raspberries

⅔ cup (*20 g*) packed fresh basil leaves, thinly sliced

½ cup (*12 g*) packed fresh mint leaves, thinly sliced

1. Cut the watermelon crosswise in half and cut off the rind. Cut the flesh into ½-inch (*1.25 cm*) cubes and place in a colander set in the sink to drain any excess liquid. Cut the skin off the pineapple and remove the core. Cut the flesh into ½-inch (*1.25 cm*) cubes and add to the colander.

2. In a dry medium skillet, toast the quinoa over high heat, gently shaking the skillet every minute or so, until the quinoa is fragrant and you can see the pieces jumping every few seconds, 3 to 4 minutes. Transfer the quinoa to a small bowl.

3. In a large bowl, combine the blueberries, blackberries, watermelon, and pineapple and stir to combine. Add the raspberries and gently stir again.

4. Divide the fruit among four bowls. Top each with the toasted quinoa, basil, and mint. Serve.

notes

HONEY-ROASTED GRAPEFRUIT
WITH PISTACHIOS

serves 4

....

A touch of honey and some heat transform grapefruit into a decadent treat, while crunchy salted pistachios provide the perfect contrast to the lightly sweetened and tender fruit. We serve this dish at brunch, but with a little extra honey it also works for dessert. If you happen to have a kitchen blowtorch, use it to give the grapefruit an extra-crispy caramelized top.

2 large red or pink grapefruit (about ¾ pound / *350 g* each), chilled

¼ cup (*60 ml*) honey

¼ cup (*35 g*) chopped toasted salted pistachios, for garnish

Fresh mint leaves, for garnish

1. Set a rack 2 to 4 inches (*5 to 10 cm*) from the oven's heat source and turn the broiler to high. Line a large plate with paper towels. Line a sheet pan with parchment paper.

2. Halve each grapefruit through the equator, then cut a thin slice off the bottom of each to create a flat surface so the grapefruit halves can sit upright. Arrange the grapefruit halves, cut-side down, on the paper towels and let stand for 5 minutes to drain a bit.

3. Using a grapefruit knife or paring knife, remove any visible seeds from the grapefruit halves, then loosen all the segments. Arrange the grapefruit halves, cut-side up, on the prepared sheet pan, drizzle evenly with the honey, and broil until the honey is bubbling and golden brown, 5 to 8 minutes.

4. Let the grapefruit halves cool slightly, then sprinkle with the pistachios and mint leaves and serve.

TIP: *Look for grapefruit that feels plump and heavy for its size, which is a good indicator the fruit is ripe.*

notes

savory starts

"Growing up, I found it impossible to follow along when my maman and grandmother baked. They would say, 'Add a pinch of salt and a dash of flour.' I couldn't keep up. I'm a recipe follower, and when I bake with my daughter, Scarlett, we measure everything, so she knows exactly what to do. I also remember loving to lick the bowl of batter, and my Scarlett is just the same!"

—MOLLY SIMS,
actress, model, and humanitarian

CRÊPES
WITH MUSHROOMS, GRUYÈRE, AND HERBES DE PROVENCE

serves 6-8

....

Ben's maman, Joelle, often made crêpes for her son's goûté, or after-school snack. These simple crêpes, made lighter thanks to some seltzer in the batter, can be filled with myriad sweet and savory ingredients and are a great way to use up leftovers. In addition to this variation, we also love the combination of ham, Swiss cheese, and herbs, as well as strawberries and Nutella and the espresso mascarpone used in our Brandy Brioche French Toast with Espresso Mascarpone (page 44). If you're making these crêpes for brunch, prep the batter and filling the night before, then cook and fill the crêpes just before serving.

CRÊPES

4 large eggs

1 cup (*240 ml*) whole milk

1 cup (*240 ml*) seltzer water

1 teaspoon sugar

½ teaspoon fine sea salt

¼ teaspoon finely ground white pepper

4 tablespoons (2 ounces / *57 g*) unsalted butter, melted

1½ cups (*218 g*) all-purpose flour

FILLING

3 tablespoons extra-virgin olive oil

2 shallots (about 4 ounces / *113 g*), thinly sliced

2 pounds (*900 g*) wild mushrooms, trimmed and roughly chopped

2 garlic cloves, minced

3 tablespoons herbes de Provence

2 teaspoons fine sea salt

1 pound (*450 g*) Gruyère cheese, shredded

Extra-virgin olive oil, for cooking the crêpes

1. MAKE THE CRÊPE BATTER: In a medium bowl, whisk together the eggs, milk, seltzer, sugar, salt, and white pepper until fully combined. While whisking, incorporate the melted butter, followed by the flour, whisking until completely smooth, about 1 minute. Transfer to an airtight container and refrigerate for at least 1 hour or overnight.

2. MAKE THE FILLING: Heat the olive oil in a large skillet over medium-high heat. When the oil is shimmering, add the shallots, reduce the heat to medium, and cook, stirring frequently, until the shallots are translucent, about 5 minutes. Add the mushrooms and cook, stirring constantly, until the mushrooms begin to soften and release their juices, 2 to 3 minutes. Reduce the heat to medium-low and add the garlic, herbes de Provence, and salt. Stir to coat the mushrooms. Continue cooking until the mushrooms are completely softened and their liquid has evaporated, 2 to 3 minutes more. Remove the pan from the heat, leaving the mushrooms in it to keep warm.

3. COOK THE CRÊPES: Set the oven to 200°F (*100°C*) to keep the crêpes warm.

4. Heat a small drizzle of olive oil in a 9-inch (*23 cm*) nonstick skillet over medium-high heat. When the oil is shimmering, ladle ¼ cup (*60 ml*) of crêpe batter into the pan, rolling the skillet around to distribute the batter across the bottom and a little bit up the sides. Continue rolling the pan until the batter is

RECIPE CONTINUES

TIP: *Store leftover batter refrigerated in an airtight container for up to 3 days.*

set, about 10 seconds. Return the pan to medium-high heat and cook the crêpe until the top is almost dry and the edges are pulling away from the skillet, about 45 seconds.

5. Flip the crêpe and quickly add about ¼ cup (*30 g*) Gruyère and about 3 tablespoons of the mushroom mixture to one side of the crêpe. Continue cooking for about 45 seconds, or until the cheese is melted. Flip the bare side of the crêpe over the cheese and mushroom filling, then fold the crêpe in half again, creating a triangle. Slide the crêpe out of the pan and onto a sheet pan to keep warm in the oven while you continue cooking, adding more oil to the pan as needed.

6. Serve immediately, or wrap the bottoms of the triangles in parchment to take these crêpes on the go.

notes

MAMAN'S BREAKFAST SANDWICH
WITH BOURBON-BACON JAM

makes 2 sandwiches

....

A staple at all maman locations, this is our spin on the classic bacon and egg breakfast sandwich. Roasted cherry tomatoes and slices of fresh avocado add layers of flavor and texture, but it's Ben's bourbon and bacon jam that really sets this sandwich apart. He created it as an alternative to the typical strips of bacon; it complements almost any egg dish and also doubles as a burger topping. You'll be very happy to have leftovers in the fridge!

½ cup (*100 g*) cherry tomatoes

3 tablespoons extra-virgin olive oil

¼ teaspoon dried thyme

Fine sea salt and freshly ground black pepper

2 (4-inch / *10 cm*) cornmeal-crusted rolls

1 cup (*300 g*) Bourbon-Bacon Jam (recipe follows)

2 large eggs

1 avocado, halved and sliced

1. Preheat the oven to 400°F (*200°C*). Line a sheet pan with parchment paper.

2. In a medium bowl, toss the cherry tomatoes with 1 tablespoon of the olive oil and the thyme. Spread in an even layer on the prepared sheet pan, season with salt and pepper, and roast until bursting, about 20 minutes. Transfer the tomatoes to a bowl and let cool. Leave the oven on; discard the parchment paper.

3. Slice open the cornmeal rolls and spread ½ cup (*150 g*) of the bourbon-bacon jam on the bottom half of each. Arrange the tops and bottoms of the rolls cut-side up on the same sheet pan and toast until the rolls are light golden brown and the bacon jam is warm, about 5 minutes.

4. Meanwhile, heat the remaining 2 tablespoons olive oil in a nonstick skillet over medium heat. When the oil is shimmering, crack the eggs into the pan, season to taste with salt and pepper, and fry until the whites are set but the yolks are still runny, about 3 minutes.

5. Place the roll bottoms on plates. Top each with a few avocado slices, a fried egg, and a few roasted cherry tomatoes. Top off the sandwiches with the roll tops and stab each through the middle with a steak knife or large toothpick to keep them together. Serve hot—and with lots of napkins.

notes

RECIPE CONTINUES

BOURBON-BACON JAM

MAKES 6 CUPS (*about 1.8 kg*)

2 pounds (*900 g*) bacon

3 yellow onions (about 2 pounds / *900 g*), diced

4 large shallots (about 6½ ounces / *180 g*), diced

11 garlic cloves, minced

2 cups (*480 ml*) bourbon

2 cups (*480 ml*) maple syrup

1 tablespoon smoked paprika

1 tablespoon chili powder

2 cups (*480 ml*) balsamic vinegar

2 cups (*340 g*) packed light brown sugar

1. Preheat the oven to 400°F (*200°C*). Line two sheet pans with parchment paper. Line two large plates with paper towels.

2. Arrange the bacon slices in a single layer on the prepared sheet pans. Bake until crispy, about 20 minutes. Transfer to the paper towels to drain and cool. Carefully pour the bacon grease into a metal or ceramic cup and let cool slightly. Chop the crispy bacon into ½-inch (*1.25 cm*) pieces and place in a 9 × 13-inch (*23 × 33 cm*) baking dish.

3. Heat 1 tablespoon of the reserved bacon fat in a large pot over medium heat; reserve the rest for another use. When the fat is shimmering, add the onions and cook, stirring frequently and covering when not stirring, until translucent, 5 to 7 minutes. Add the shallots and garlic and cook, stirring frequently and covering when not stirring, until the onions start sticking to the pot, about 15 minutes.

4. Uncover and continue cooking, stirring frequently, until the onions are browned and really sticking to the pot, about 35 minutes more.

5. Add the bourbon and deglaze the pot, using a wooden spoon to scrape up any browned bits off the bottom. Add the maple syrup, smoked paprika, and chili powder and bring to a boil. Cook, stirring frequently, until as thick as gravy, about 5 minutes. Add the balsamic vinegar and brown sugar and simmer, stirring every 5 minutes and adjusting the heat as needed, until thick and reduced by half, about 1 hour.

6. Remove the pot from the heat and let cool for 10 minutes. Pour the cooled mixture over the bacon and stir to coat. Let stand at room temperature, stirring occasionally, until cool to the touch, about 1 hour. Cover and refrigerate until thick and completely cool, at least 2 hours.

TIP: *Store refrigerated in an airtight container for up to 7 days.*

PROVENÇAL EGGS RATATOUILLE

serves 4-8

(4 servings for 2 eggs per person; 8 servings for 1 egg per person)

....

This end-of-summer Provençal classic reminds Ben of trips to the local market with his maman to buy fresh produce like eggplant, zucchini, and tomatoes. For deeper flavor, we roast the vegetables before cooking the mixture on the stove. We bake eggs right into the stew and add a sprinkle of feta to create a full breakfast feast, but you can serve the ratatouille with just toast for a lighter meal. If you don't have a large enameled cast-iron skillet, make the stew in a large pot and transfer it to a 9-inch (*23 cm*) pie plate to bake the eggs. You can also bake it in mini (6-inch / *15 cm*) cast-iron skillets for individual servings.

1 small eggplant (about ¾ pound / *340 g*), diced

¾ cup (*180 ml*) extra-virgin olive oil

Fine sea salt and freshly ground black pepper

2 zucchini (about 1¼ pounds / *560 g*), diced

1 yellow onion (about 11 ounces / *310 g*), diced

1 (12-ounce / *340 g*) jar roasted red peppers, drained and roughly chopped

3 garlic cloves, minced

5 teaspoons dried thyme

½ teaspoon crushed red pepper flakes

1 (28-ounce / *785 g*) can crushed San Marzano tomatoes

⅔ cup (*20 g*) packed fresh basil leaves, chopped

8 large eggs

8 slices country bread or baguette

3 ounces (*84 g*) herbed sheep's milk feta cheese, crumbled

¼ cup (*15 g*) sliced scallions (optional)

1. Preheat the oven to 400°F (*200°C*). Line two sheet pans with parchment paper.

2. In a medium bowl, toss the eggplant with 3 tablespoons of the olive oil and a pinch of salt, then spread in an even layer on one of the prepared sheet pans. In the same bowl, toss the zucchini with 3 tablespoons of the olive oil and a pinch of salt, then spread in an even layer on the other prepared sheet pan. Roast together for about 25 minutes, or until the eggplant and zucchini are lightly browned. Remove from the oven and set aside. Increase the oven temperature to 450°F (*230°C*).

3. Meanwhile, heat ¼ cup (*60 ml*) of the olive oil in a 12-inch (*30 cm*) enameled cast-iron skillet over medium heat. When the oil is shimmering, add the onion and cook until softened, about 5 minutes. Add the roasted peppers, garlic, thyme, pepper flakes, 1 teaspoon salt, and ¼ teaspoon black pepper. Stir well and cook until the onions are translucent, about 2 minutes more. Add the tomatoes and their juices, stir to combine, and bring to a simmer. Continue simmering, stirring occasionally and adjusting the heat as needed, until the sauce thickens and darkens in color, 10 to 15 minutes.

4. Add the roasted eggplant and zucchini, along with the basil, stir to combine, and simmer for 5 minutes more to let the flavors meld.

5. Remove the skillet from the heat and use a spoon to create 8 evenly spaced wells on the surface of the ratatouille. Crack an egg into each of the wells, then transfer to the oven and bake until the egg whites are just set but the yolks are still runny,

12 minutes—the eggs will continue to cook as the ratatouille rests, so remove the skillet from the oven when they still look a bit underdone. Let the ratatouille stand for 5 minutes and turn the oven to broil.

6. Brush the bread with the remaining 2 tablespoons olive oil, arrange on a sheet pan, and broil until golden brown, 1 to 2 minutes.

7. Sprinkle the ratatouille with the feta and scallions (if using) and serve family-style with the toasted bread alongside for dipping.

SMOKED SALMON BOWL
WITH AVOCADO AND WAFFLE-IRON HASH BROWNS

serves 4

Ben loves smoked salmon, but he wanted to find a way to serve it with something less expected than bagels and cream cheese. Well, this dish is now our number one seller across all maman locations! While it's definitely a salad with plenty of greens, avocado, and cucumber, the hash browns and smoked salmon make it a hearty and well-balanced meal—and you can make it even more substantial by adding 6-minute boiled eggs, like we do at the restaurant, or a dollop of crème fraîche. Hash browns are quick and effortless in a waffle iron. Plus, they freeze well and make an excellent side for a variety of dishes. In other words, you may want to make extra.

HASH BROWNS

4 medium russet potatoes (about 2½ pounds / *1.1 kg*), peeled (see Tip)

1 stick (4 ounces / *113 g*) unsalted butter, melted

2 teaspoons dried thyme

2 teaspoons fine sea salt

½ teaspoon freshly ground black pepper

Vegetable oil spray

SALAD

5 ounces (*140 g*) mixed greens

¼ cup (*60 ml*) Balsamic Vinaigrette (page 125) or store-bought

2 avocados, halved and sliced

1 English cucumber (about 10 ounces / *280 g*), sliced

8 ounces (*225 g*) smoked salmon (such as Ducktrap River of Maine)

1 lemon, quartered

4 fresh dill sprigs

notes

1. **MAKE THE HASH BROWNS:** Set the oven to 200°F (*100°C*) to keep the hash browns warm. Heat a waffle iron according to the manufacturer's instructions.

2. Cut the potatoes into long, thin strips. In a food processor fitted with the shredding disk (see Tip), shred the potatoes, then transfer to a large bowl. Add the melted butter, thyme, salt, and pepper and toss to coat. Transfer the mixture to a colander set in the sink. Press a piece of plastic wrap onto the surface of the potatoes to prevent browning and let drain for at least 5 minutes and up to 15 minutes.

3. Coat the hot waffle iron generously with vegetable oil spray. Using your hands, grab one-quarter of the potato mixture, squeeze out any remaining liquid, then carefully press it onto the waffle iron, spreading it to cover the entire surface. Close the iron and cook until golden brown and crispy, 15 to 20 minutes—the hash browns are ready when you can easily remove them from the iron without them falling apart. Keep warm in the oven while you cook the remaining hash browns, spraying the waffle iron each time.

4. **MAKE THE SALAD:** In a large bowl, toss the mixed greens with the vinaigrette until well coated, then divide among four bowls. Fan avocado and cucumber slices on opposite sides of each bowl. Halve the hash browns diagonally and arrange in the center of each bowl. Arrange some smoked salmon on top of the hash browns in each bowl, layering to create height. Garnish each bowl with a lemon wedge and a sprig of fresh dill and serve.

TIPS:

You can use any potatoes to make these hash browns, but we favor russets because they get crispy on the outside but stay light and fluffy on the inside for the perfect bite.

If you don't want to get out the food processor, use the large holes of a box grater to shred the peeled potatoes.

Store hash browns well wrapped and refrigerated for up to 1 day; reheat in a skillet with a bit of olive oil to warm and crisp before serving.

ROASTED POTATOES AND BRUSSELS SPROUTS

WITH WHIPPED RICOTTA, OLIVE-CAPER GREMOLATA, AND A SUNNY EGG

serves 4

....

Potatoes and eggs are a classic combination, and while this dish is on our breakfast menu, we could easily eat it any time of the day—and any day of the year (in spring and summer, we swap asparagus for the Brussels sprouts). Mild, meaty Castelvetrano olives really complete this dish, so they are worth seeking out, but any unstuffed green olive will do. To make this vegetarian dish vegan, swap the egg and ricotta for avocado. Alternatively, you can crisp thin slices of prosciutto in the oven and layer them on top. You'll have plenty of leftover gremolata, which will shine on other veggie and egg dishes, as well as on sandwiches and steak.

1½ pounds (*675 g*) fingerling potatoes

6 tablespoons (*90 ml*) extra-virgin olive oil

Fine sea salt and freshly ground black pepper

1 pound (*450 g*) Brussels sprouts

½ red onion (about 5½ ounces / *154 g*), thinly sliced

1 cup (*226 g*) whole-milk ricotta cheese

4 large eggs

1⅓ cups (*304 g*) Olive-Caper Gremolata (recipe follows)

Fresh dill sprigs, for garnish (optional)

notes

1. Preheat the oven to 400°F (*200°C*). Line two sheet pans with parchment paper.

2. Cut any large potatoes into quarters, cut any smaller potatoes lengthwise in half, and leave any really small ones whole; you want pieces that are all about the same size. In a large bowl, toss the potatoes with 2 tablespoons of the olive oil and 1 teaspoon salt. Spread in an even layer on one of the prepared sheet pans and roast until tender and golden brown, 35 to 40 minutes.

3. Meanwhile, trim the ends off the Brussels sprouts. Cut any large ones into quarters and cut the rest in half. In a large bowl, toss the Brussels sprouts and red onion with 2 tablespoons of the olive oil and 1 teaspoon salt. Spread in an even layer on the other prepared sheet pan and roast alongside the potatoes until browned and a little crispy, about 30 minutes.

4. In a small bowl, whisk the ricotta with ¼ teaspoon salt to lighten, about 1 minute. Scrape down the sides of the bowl and whisk for 10 seconds more.

5. Transfer the roasted vegetables to a large bowl and toss to combine.

6. Heat the remaining 2 tablespoons olive oil in a large nonstick skillet over medium heat. When the oil is shimmering, crack the eggs into the pan, season with some salt and pepper, and fry until the whites are set but the yolks are still runny, about 3 minutes.

RECIPE CONTINUES

7. Divide the vegetables among four plates or bowls. Arrange a dollop of whipped ricotta in the center of each plate and top with a fried egg, followed by the gremolata. Garnish with fresh dill sprigs, if desired, and serve.

OLIVE-CAPER GREMOLATA

MAKES 2½ CUPS (*570 g*)

2 cups (*50 g*) packed fresh parsley leaves

½ cup (*13 g*) packed fresh dill leaves

½ cup (*83 g*) drained capers

2 cups (*250 g*) pitted Castelvetrano olives or other unstuffed green olives

½ cup (*120 ml*) extra-virgin olive oil

1 tablespoon fresh lemon juice

¼ teaspoon fine sea salt

¼ teaspoon freshly ground black pepper

1. In a food processor, combine the parsley and dill and process until the leaves are finely chopped, about 1 minute. Transfer to a medium bowl.

2. Add the capers to the food processor and pulse 3 to 5 times to roughly chop. Add to the herb mixture. Add the olives to the food processor and pulse 3 to 5 times to roughly chop. Add to the herb mixture.

3. Add the olive oil, lemon juice, salt, and pepper to the herb mixture and stir to combine—the gremolata should be an oily, chunky mixture.

TIP: *Store the gremolata refrigerated in an airtight container for up to 7 days.*

notes

when maman says ...

Our favorite recipe sources will always be our mamans and grandmothers, but like many home cooks and bakers, they cook their best dishes from memory. They've made and remade these cakes and quiches and soups so many times that they don't need to look at a list of ingredients or follow a written set of steps.

Knowing a dish so well is a beautiful thing, but when the details are vague or there's no tangible recipe at all, it's that much harder to pass on to the next generation. When grandma says to add a pinch or smidgen, what does that really mean? We've updated our family recipes to include standard teaspoons and tablespoons, and along the way we created a legend to spell out just what it means to add a dash or splash to a recipe—we even figured out the measurement equivalent for a yogurt container (see Joelle's Yogurt Loaf, page 69). If your family is like ours, you likely have a bunch of passed-down recipes you struggle to get just right or that are too imprecise to even try. Hopefully, these "translations" will help!

A DASH is equal to ⅛ teaspoon, an amount so small you don't need to use a measuring spoon.

JUST A PINCH means the amount you can pinch between your fingers, and usually falls somewhere between ¹⁄₁₆ and ⅛ teaspoon, so a little less than a dash.

A SMIDGEN is the smallest of measurements, equal to half a pinch, or ¹⁄₃₂ teaspoon. In other words, it's a very small amount!

A SPLASH is used for liquids and varies depending on what you're making. For baking, adding a splash would mean about 1 teaspoon, while for cooking on the stove, a splash would be closer to ¼ cup.

JUST A DROP equals ¹⁄₆₄ teaspoon, or the absolute smallest amount of liquid you can add.

HEIRLOOM TOMATO AND SAUSAGE CASSEROLE

serves 6-8

You'll find an abundance of leftover baguettes in any French household—and ours is no exception. Extra bread is perfect for breakfast casseroles like this sausage and tomato-studded version. You have to make it at least 6 hours in advance, so it's ideal for holiday brunches—just pop it in the oven in the morning for an easy family feast. For a more striking presentation, use different colored tomatoes—vine-ripened ones will be best in winter—and to make it vegetarian, swap the sausage for sautéed mushrooms.

Vegetable oil spray

2 tablespoons extra-virgin olive oil

1 pound (*450 g*) sweet or hot Italian sausage, casings removed

1 large or 2 medium leeks (about 10 ounces / *280 g*), cut into rings and well washed (see Tip)

2 garlic cloves, minced

¼ baguette (about 6 inches / *15 cm*), cut into large chunks

¼ cup (*5 g*) packed fresh oregano leaves

½ cup (*36 g*) packed sliced fresh chives

1 cup (*100 g*) grated Parmesan cheese

8 large eggs

1½ cups (*360 ml*) half-and-half

Fine sea salt and freshly ground black pepper

3 large heirloom tomatoes (about 1¼ pounds / *560 g*), thinly sliced

¼ cup (*8 g*) packed sliced fresh basil leaves

1 cup (*200 g*) Basil Pesto (page 127) or store-bought

notes

1. Line a large plate with paper towels. Coat a 9 × 13-inch (*23 × 33 cm*) baking dish with vegetable oil spray.

2. Heat the olive oil in a large skillet over medium heat. When the oil is shimmering, add the sausage and cook, breaking it up with a wooden spoon, until beginning to brown, about 3 minutes. Add the leeks and garlic and continue cooking until the leeks are softened and the sausage is cooked through, 5 to 8 minutes. Using a slotted spoon, transfer the sausage mixture to the prepared plate to drain.

3. In a large bowl, combine the chunks of baguette, the sausage mixture, oregano, ¼ cup (*18 g*) of the chives, and ½ cup (*50 g*) of the Parmesan. Toss to combine. Spread the sausage mixture evenly in the prepared baking dish.

4. In a medium bowl, whisk together the eggs, half-and-half, and 1 teaspoon each salt and pepper. Pour the egg mixture over the sausage mixture, gently pushing down to submerge the sausage and bread. Tightly cover the baking dish with plastic wrap, then place a few plates or other heavy objects on top of the plastic wrap to compress the ingredients. Refrigerate, weighted, for at least 6 hours or overnight.

5. Preheat the oven to 350°F (*180°C*).

6. Remove the baking dish from the refrigerator and uncover. Layer the tomatoes across the top of the casserole, overlapping them. Season with salt and pepper, then sprinkle the remaining ½ cup (*50 g*) Parmesan over top.

7. Bake until set, about 40 minutes.

8. Let the casserole rest for 10 minutes, then cut into 6 to 8 portions and sprinkle with the remaining ¼ cup (18 g) chives and the sliced basil. Serve with the pesto.

TIPS:

Leeks can be quite dirty, and cleaning them requires a bit of extra care. Cut off and discard the hairy root ends and dark green tops of the leeks. Peel off and discard the first outer layer and cut the leeks crosswise into rings. Thoroughly wash the cut leeks in a large bowl of water to remove any dirt.

Store the casserole well wrapped and refrigerated for up to 3 days; warm individual slices in a 400°F (200°C) oven for 10 minutes.

JOELLE'S YOGURT LOAF

WITH SUN-DRIED TOMATOES, OLIVES, AND GOAT CHEESE

makes one 9×5-inch (23×12.5 cm) loaf

Ben's maman, Joelle, makes several variations of this yogurt-enriched loaf—it's a family favorite. The yogurt makes it incredibly moist, and to keep cleanup super easy, Joelle uses the yogurt container as her measuring tool, a trick we've found in many passed-down recipes (see When Maman Says . . . , page 65). We've converted everything to real measurements, but when Joelle shared the recipe, most of the ingredients were listed by the number of yogurt container scoops she uses! You can swap in other savory ingredients like ham, Gruyère, and roasted red peppers. Serve this loaf on its own or toasted with butter.

Olive oil, for the pan

1½ cups (*218 g*) all-purpose flour

1 tablespoon baking powder

½ teaspoon freshly ground black pepper

3 large eggs

½ cup (*120 g*) plain yogurt

½ cup (*120 ml*) extra-virgin olive oil

½ cup (*100 g*) chopped oil-packed sun-dried tomatoes, drained

½ cup (*60 g*) sliced pitted black olives

½ cup (*80 g*) crumbled goat cheese

1. Set a rack in the center of the oven and preheat to 350°F (*180°C*). Grease a 9 × 5-inch (*23 × 12.5 cm*) loaf pan with olive oil.

2. In a medium bowl, whisk together the flour, baking powder, and pepper.

3. In a stand mixer fitted with the paddle attachment, beat the eggs on low for about 30 seconds to break up the yolks. With the mixer still running on low, add the yogurt, followed by the olive oil, and beat for about 45 seconds to combine. With the mixer still on low, gradually add the flour mixture in small batches and mix, scraping down the sides of the bowl, until fully combined, about 2 minutes total. Add the sun-dried tomatoes, olives, and goat cheese and using a rubber spatula, fold until just incorporated. Be careful not to overmix the batter; you want the cheese to stay in pieces.

4. Transfer the batter to the prepared pan and bake until a toothpick inserted into the center comes out clean, 30 to 35 minutes.

5. Set the pan on a wire rack and let cool for about 20 minutes, then invert the loaf onto the rack. Flip the loaf again so it is right-side up and enjoy warm or let cool slightly.

TIP: *Store the loaf in the refrigerator tightly wrapped in plastic wrap for up to 3 days.*

notes

MAMAN'S RABBIT HOLE
BREAKFAST BREAD BOWL

serves 4

....

Rabbits are a theme at maman. You'll find them on our shelves, in the toile pattern on our to-go boxes and cups, and even in our wallpaper. There's no rabbit in this recipe, but our favorite animal seemed like a fitting alternative to the "toad" part of "toad in a hole," the classic English dish that inspires this one. In lieu of sausage, we use pastrami, but you can skip the meat to make this vegetarian. Our rabbit hole also takes inspiration from pain surprise, a traditional French dish of hollowed-out and stuffed bread. (The bread you scoop out of the rolls is perfect to save for bread crumbs.) If you're entertaining, prep the stuffed rolls ahead, refrigerate them for up to 2 days, and then bake them off once guests arrive.

---

5 tablespoons (*75 ml*) extra-virgin olive oil

2 yellow onions (about 1⅓ pounds / *620 g*), thinly sliced

1 tablespoon balsamic vinegar

2 vine-ripened tomatoes (about 9 ounces / *252 g*), thickly sliced

⅛ teaspoon dried thyme

Fine sea salt and freshly ground black pepper

4 medium to large cornmeal- or sesame-crusted rolls

8 slices pastrami

5 ounces (*140 g*) Comté or Gruyère cheese, shredded

4 large eggs

1 cup (*40 g*) packed baby arugula

notes

_____

_____

_____

_____

_____

_____

1. Heat 2 tablespoons of the olive oil in a large nonstick skillet over medium heat. When the oil is shimmering, add the onions and cook, stirring frequently and covering when not stirring, until soft and translucent, about 10 minutes.

2. Reduce the heat to medium-low and continue to cook, stirring frequently and covering when not stirring, until the onions are browned and sticking to the pan, about 35 minutes.

3. Add the balsamic vinegar and deglaze the pan, using a wooden spoon to scrape up any browned bits. Continue to cook, stirring frequently, until the vinegar has been absorbed and the skillet is almost dry, about 10 minutes. Remove the pan from the heat and transfer the onions to a small bowl.

4. Meanwhile, preheat the oven to 350°F (*180°C*). Line a small baking dish with parchment paper. Line a sheet pan with parchment paper.

5. Arrange the tomatoes in overlapping layers in the bottom of the prepared baking dish. Drizzle with 1 tablespoon of the olive oil and sprinkle with the thyme, ⅛ teaspoon salt, and ⅛ teaspoon pepper. Bake until very soft, about 25 minutes. Transfer to a medium bowl and let cool. Increase the oven temperature to 400°F (*200°C*).

6. Slice a small portion off the top of each roll and set the tops aside. Using your hands, gently dig out the inside of each roll, creating a hole at least 1½ inches (*3.75 cm*) deep and 2 inches (*5 cm*) wide (save the insides for another use). Line the sides and bottom of each hole with 2 slices of pastrami, followed by 2 slices of roasted tomato. Divide the

caramelized onions and shredded Comté among the rolls. Arrange the stuffed rolls on the prepared sheet pan and bake for about 5 minutes. Add the reserved tops of the rolls, cut-side down, to the sheet pan and bake until the filling is warm and the cheese is fully melted, 3 to 5 minutes more.

7. Meanwhile, heat the remaining 2 tablespoons olive oil in a nonstick skillet over medium heat. When the oil is shimmering, crack the eggs into the pan, season with some salt and pepper, and fry until the whites are set but the yolks are still runny, about 3 minutes.

8. Place each rabbit hole on a plate. Lightly stuff some baby arugula into each, then top with a fried egg and a toasted bun top and serve.

MARION'S ZUCCHINI BREAD
WITH CHEDDAR AND LEEKS

makes one 9×5-inch (23×12.5 cm) loaf

This Cheddar and leek–infused zucchini loaf is a savory spin on a recipe from the grandmother of our marketing director, Andrea DeMaio Szot. They used to bake it together using a handwritten recipe card. We like to serve the maman version toasted with a little butter or our Bourbon-Bacon Jam (page 56). Beyond breakfast and afternoon snacks, this zucchini loaf makes an excellent predinner bite, especially when served with an aperitif.

Olive oil, for the pan

¼ cup plus 2 teaspoons (*70 ml*) extra-virgin olive oil

1 leek (about 5 ounces / *140 g*), cut into rings and well washed (see Tip, page 67)

Fine sea salt and freshly ground black pepper

3 cups (*435 g*) all-purpose flour

2 tablespoons chopped fresh rosemary needles

1 tablespoon baking powder

1 teaspoon baking soda

½ teaspoon grated nutmeg

¾ cup (*180 ml*) whole milk

1 tablespoon apple cider vinegar

3 large eggs

1½ cups (*200 g*) grated zucchini (about 1 zucchini)

8 ounces (*225 g*) sharp white Cheddar cheese, shredded

Butter or Bourbon-Bacon Jam (page 56), for serving (optional)

notes

1. Set a rack in the center of the oven and preheat to 350°F (*180°C*). Grease a 9 × 5-inch (*23 × 12.5 cm*) loaf pan with olive oil.

2. Heat 2 teaspoons of the olive oil in a small skillet over medium-low heat. When the oil is shimmering, add the leek, season with salt, and cook, stirring occasionally, until soft, about 5 minutes. Transfer to a small bowl.

3. In a medium bowl, whisk together the flour, rosemary, baking powder, baking soda, nutmeg, 2 teaspoons salt, and 1 teaspoon pepper.

4. In a liquid measuring cup, combine the milk and apple cider vinegar and let stand to curdle.

5. In a stand mixer fitted with the paddle attachment, beat the eggs on low. With the mixer still running on low, slowly drizzle in the curdled milk, followed by the remaining ¼ cup (*60 ml*) olive oil. Add the grated zucchini. With the mixer still on low, gradually add the flour mixture in small batches. Scrape down the sides of the bowl, then add the shredded Cheddar and the sautéed leeks. Beat on medium for 15 seconds, then scrape down the sides of the bowl and beat on medium for about 30 seconds more to fully combine.

6. Transfer the batter to the prepared pan and bake until a skewer inserted into the center of the loaf comes out clean, 1 hour to 1 hour 5 minutes.

7. Let the loaf cool in the pan for about 20 minutes, then invert onto a wire rack. Flip the loaf again so it is right-side up and let cool slightly. Cut into thick slices and serve as is, or toasted with butter or bourbon-bacon jam.

TIP: *Store the zucchini bread at room temperature tightly wrapped in plastic wrap for up to 3 days.*

saucisson pasta salad
(page 124)

phyllis salad
(page 119)

potato, leek and sunchoke
soup (page 144)

PART II

All-Day Café

quiche esther
(page 83)

quiches and savory tarts

"My maman's cooking absolutely comes from a place
of love to nurture her children and grandchildren.
Nothing gives her greater joy than watching her
grandchildren eat her food."

—SHELLEY KLEYN ARMISTEAD,
partner and COO, Gjelina Group

TIP:
Store pastry dough tightly wrapped in plastic wrap and refrigerated for up to 1 week or frozen for up to 1 month. Thaw before rolling. You can also roll the dough, fit it into a tart pan, and freeze it, well wrapped in plastic wrap, for up to 1 month. Use straight from the freezer without thawing.

CLASSIC PASTRY DOUGH

Makes enough for three 9½-inch (24 cm) round pastry shells or
three 14 × 5-inch (35 × 12.5 cm) rectangular pastry shells

....

We make dozens of batches of this versatile dough every week, as it can be used for almost any sweet or savory tart and can also be refrigerated or frozen. Elisa's maman freezes her dough in disposable foil tart pans, so she always has some on hand. It's fun to get kids involved in rolling out the dough. Outside of licking batters off of spatulas, that was Elisa's favorite kitchen activity as a child. Use this for all our quiches, our Summer Vegetable Spiral Tart (page 87), and our Cherry Tomato, Caramelized Onion, and Feta Tart (page 88).

4⅓ cups (*625 g*) all-purpose flour

1 tablespoon plus 1 teaspoon fine sea salt

2 sticks plus 6 tablespoons (11 ounces / *310 g*) cold unsalted butter, cubed

2 large eggs, beaten

1¼ cups (*300 ml*) ice-cold water

1. In a stand mixer fitted with the paddle attachment, stir together the flour and salt. With the mixer running on low, gradually add the butter, then continue mixing until most of the butter is in pea-sized pieces, about 5 minutes. Add the eggs and mix until incorporated. With the mixer still on low, drizzle in the ice-cold water and continue mixing until a very smooth dough forms, about 30 seconds.

2. Turn out the dough onto a lightly floured surface and shape it into a ball—it should be very soft but not sticky. Divide the dough into 3 equal portions. Shape each portion into a tight disk ½ inch (*1.25 cm*) thick, wrap in plastic wrap, and refrigerate for at least 1 hour before using.

3. **TO MAKE A ROUND TART OR QUICHE SHELL:** On a lightly floured surface, use a rolling pin to roll 1 disk of dough into a 12-inch (*30 cm*) round. Carefully roll the dough around the rolling pin, brushing off any excess flour. Unroll the dough over a 9½-inch (*24 cm*) round plain or scalloped tart pan.

TO MAKE A RECTANGULAR TART SHELL: On a lightly floured surface, use a rolling pin to roll 1 disk of dough into a 16 × 7-inch (*40 × 17.5 cm*) rectangle. Carefully roll the dough around the rolling pin, brushing off any excess flour. Unroll the dough over a 14 × 5-inch (*35 × 12.5 cm*) rectangular plain or scalloped tart pan.

4. **FOR BOTH:** Gently tuck the dough into the edges of the pan, using a floured finger to press the dough into each curve and letting excess dough fall over the edge. Roll the rolling pin across the top of the tart pan to cut the dough around the edges, then gently pull the excess dough away to leave a clean edge. Freeze for at least 15 minutes.

notes

QUICHE CAITLIN
WITH ASPARAGUS, FETA, AND DILL

serves 6-8

We named this light and colorful quiche for its biggest fan, our beverage director, Caitlin Burke. The combination of asparagus, feta, and dill makes it perfect for a spring brunch. We leave the asparagus raw, because the slightly crunchy texture contrasts beautifully with the soft egg and cheese filling. If you don't have dill, parsley is a great alternative.

1 disk Classic Pastry Dough (page 79) or store-bought pie dough

6 large eggs, beaten

2 cups (*480 ml*) half-and-half

½ teaspoon grated nutmeg

½ teaspoon fine sea salt

½ teaspoon freshly ground black pepper

1 large bunch asparagus (about ¾ pound / *340 g*), trimmed and cut into 1-inch (*2.5 cm*) pieces

½ cup (*30 g*) sliced scallions

1 cup (*150 g*) crumbled feta cheese

½ cup (*13 g*) packed chopped fresh dill

1. Roll out the dough and fit it into a 9½-inch (*24 cm*) round plain or scalloped tart pan as directed on page 79. Freeze for at least 15 minutes.

2. Set a rack in the center of the oven and preheat to 350°F (*180°C*). Line a sheet pan with parchment paper.

3. In a medium bowl, whisk together the eggs, half-and-half, nutmeg, salt, and pepper until fully combined.

4. Remove the tart shell from the freezer and set the pan on the prepared sheet pan. Scatter the asparagus, scallions, and feta evenly across the bottom of the pastry shell. Whisk the dill into the egg mixture, then slowly pour it over the vegetables and cheese.

5. Carefully transfer the sheet pan to the oven and bake until lightly browned around the edges and set in the center, about 1 hour. To test, give the sheet pan a gentle shake—the quiche shouldn't wobble at all.

6. Let cool for 30 minutes, then remove from the pan, slice, and serve.

TIP: *Store the quiche wrapped in plastic and refrigerated for up to 3 days. Reheat in a 400°F (200°C) oven for 7 to 10 minutes.*

notes

QUICHE ESTHER
WITH BUTTERNUT SQUASH AND KALE

serves 6-8

....

This veggie-packed quiche is named for Esther Laseur, one of our favorite marketing interns of all time—she loved its hearty combination of squash and kale, lightly sweetened with maple syrup. Quiche can be made ahead and travels well, making it ideal for potlucks or brunch at your in-laws' house. You can use mustard greens or arugula instead of baby kale, and acorn or any firm squash in place of the butternut squash—just be sure to roast it, as that's the secret to bringing out its natural sweetness.

1 disk Classic Pastry Dough (page 79) or store-bought pie dough

1 small butternut squash (about 1½ pounds / *675 g*), peeled and cut into 1-inch (*2.5 cm*) cubes

3 tablespoons maple syrup

2 tablespoons extra-virgin olive oil

1 teaspoon grated nutmeg

1 teaspoon fine sea salt

6 large eggs, beaten

2 cups (*480 ml*) half-and-half

½ teaspoon freshly ground black pepper

1½ cups (*60 g*) packed baby kale

notes

1. Roll out the dough and fit it into a 9½-inch (*24 cm*) round plain or scalloped tart pan as directed on page 79. Freeze for at least 15 minutes.

2. Set a rack in the center of the oven and preheat to 350°F (*180°C*). Line a sheet pan with parchment paper.

3. In a large bowl, combine the butternut squash, maple syrup, olive oil, ½ teaspoon of the nutmeg, and ½ teaspoon of the salt and toss to coat. Spread in an even layer on the prepared sheet pan and bake until easily pierced with a fork, about 20 minutes. Transfer to a bowl to cool. Leave the oven on and line the sheet pan with clean parchment paper.

4. In a medium bowl, whisk together the eggs, half-and-half, pepper, and the remaining ½ teaspoon nutmeg and ½ teaspoon salt until fully combined.

5. Remove the tart shell from the freezer and set the pan on the prepared sheet pan. Scatter half of the baby kale and all of the butternut squash across the bottom of the shell. Slowly pour the egg mixture over the top. Scatter the remaining baby kale across the top, gently pressing the leaves into the liquid.

6. Carefully transfer the sheet pan to the oven and bake until the quiche is lightly browned around the edges and set in the center, 40 to 45 minutes. To test, give the sheet pan a gentle shake—the quiche shouldn't wobble at all.

7. Let cool for 30 minutes, then remove from the pan, slice, and serve.

TIP: *Store the quiche wrapped in plastic and refrigerated for up to 3 days. Reheat in a 400°F (200°C) oven for 7 to 10 minutes.*

QUICHE LORRAINE
WITH PARISIAN HAM AND COMTÉ

serves 6-8

In Ben's family's household, and throughout France, quiche is enjoyed for breakfast, lunch, and dinner. Quiche Lorraine originated in the Lorraine region of France, and is named for the area's unique dialect, a mix of French and German—quiche actually means "cake" in this dialect. This crowd-pleasing classic, studded with ham and cheese, is one of maman's bestsellers; we even make mini versions for events. Parisian ham is also known as jambon de Paris; if you can't find it, use slow-cooked deli ham.

1 disk Classic Pastry Dough (page 79) or store-bought pie dough

6 large eggs, beaten

2 cups (*480 ml*) half-and-half

½ teaspoon grated nutmeg

½ teaspoon fine sea salt

½ teaspoon freshly ground black pepper

7 ounces (*200 g*) Parisian ham (jambon de Paris) or slow-cooked deli ham, cut into ½-inch (*1.25 cm*) pieces (see Tip, page 95)

8½ ounces (*240 g*) Comté or Gruyère cheese, shredded

1. Roll out the dough and fit it into a 9½-inch (*24 cm*) round plain or scalloped tart pan as directed on page 79. Freeze for at least 15 minutes.

2. Set a rack in the center of the oven and preheat to 350°F (*180°C*). Line a sheet pan with parchment paper.

3. In a medium bowl, whisk together the eggs, half-and-half, nutmeg, salt, and pepper until fully combined.

4. Remove the tart shell from the freezer and set the pan on the prepared sheet pan. Scatter the ham and Comté across the bottom of the pastry shell. Slowly pour the egg mixture over the top.

5. Carefully transfer the sheet pan to the oven and bake until browned around the edges and set in the center, about 1 hour 5 minutes. To test, give the sheet pan a gentle shake—the quiche shouldn't wobble at all.

6. Let cool for 30 minutes, then remove from the pan, slice, and serve.

TIP: *Store the quiche wrapped in plastic and refrigerated for up to 3 days. Reheat in a 400°F (200°C) oven for 7 to 10 minutes.*

notes

SUMMER VEGETABLE SPIRAL TART

serves 6-8

....

Thinly sliced summer vegetables make this tart as delicious as it is beautiful. Creating the stunning visual effect takes a bit of extra effort—use the finest setting on a mandoline or press hard with a Y-shaped peeler to create the thin strips of vegetables—but it is so worth it. This colorful tart will impress guests at brunch, lunch, or dinner—just add a simple green salad or, even better, our Julia Salad: Cumin Chickpea Salad with Roasted Red Peppers, Feta, and Scallions (page 128).

1 disk Classic Pastry Dough (page 79) or store-bought pie dough

2 zucchini (about 1¼ pounds / 560 g), cut into very thin strips

3 large carrots (about 15 ounces / 420 g), cut into very thin strips

1 large eggplant (about 1 pound / 450 g), cut into very thin strips

½ cup (120 ml) extra-virgin olive oil

2 teaspoons herbes de Provence

½ teaspoon fine sea salt

½ teaspoon freshly ground black pepper

2 cups (400 g) Basil Pesto (page 127) or store-bought

1. Roll out the dough and fit it into a 9½-inch (24 cm) round plain or scalloped tart pan as directed on page 79. Freeze for at least 15 minutes.

2. Set a rack in the center of the oven and preheat to 350°F (180°C). Line a sheet pan with parchment paper.

3. In a large bowl, combine the zucchini, carrots, and eggplant. Add the olive oil, herbes de Provence, salt, and pepper and toss to coat the vegetables.

4. Remove the tart shell from the freezer and set the pan on the prepared sheet pan. Using the back of a spoon, spread 1 cup (200 g) pesto evenly across the bottom of the tart shell.

5. Starting on the outside edge of the pan, layer strips of vegetables in a tight, overlapping spiral, alternating vegetables to create a colorful pattern and building toward the center of the pastry shell, until you've used all of the vegetables and filled the pastry shell. Bake for about 30 minutes, or until browned around the edges.

6. Slice and serve, drizzling each piece with the remaining pesto or serving it alongside in a bowl.

TIP:
Store the tart wrapped in plastic and refrigerated for up to 5 days. Reheat in a 400°F (200°C) oven for 7 to 10 minutes.

notes

CHERRY TOMATO, CARAMELIZED ONION, AND FETA TART

serves 4

You will always find cherry tomatoes in our kitchen, especially multicolored. These tiny tomatoes are bursting with flavor and can be added to pasta, tarts, or salads. Here, we combine this sweet staple with feta and caramelized onions made extra rich by a splash of red wine. We caramelize the onions quickly to minimize prep, but you can take the longer, more traditional approach used for Maman's Rabbit Hole Breakfast Bread Bowl (page 70).

1 disk Classic Pastry Dough (page 79) or store-bought pie dough

2 tablespoons extra-virgin olive oil

1 red onion (about 11 ounces / 310 g), thinly sliced

1 garlic clove, minced

1 tablespoon dry red wine

1 cup (150 g) crumbled feta cheese

¼ cup (60 ml) heavy cream

1¾ cups (350 g) cherry tomatoes, preferably multicolored, halved

1 tablespoon fresh thyme leaves

½ teaspoon fine sea salt

½ teaspoon freshly ground black pepper

TIP: *Store the tart wrapped in plastic and refrigerated for up to 2 days. Reheat in a 400°F (200°C) oven for 7 to 10 minutes.*

notes

1. Roll out the dough and fit it into a 14 × 5-inch (35 × 12.5 cm) rectangular plain or scalloped tart pan as directed on page 79. Freeze for at least 15 minutes.

2. Set a rack in the center of the oven and preheat to 350°F (180°C). Line a sheet pan with parchment paper.

3. Heat the olive oil in a small nonstick skillet over medium heat. When the oil is shimmering, add the red onion and cook, stirring frequently, until soft and translucent, about 10 minutes. If the onion sticks to the bottom of the pan, add a few tablespoons of water to deglaze the pan, using a wooden spoon to scrape any bits off the bottom. Add the garlic and cook, stirring frequently, for about 1 minute. Reduce the heat to medium-low, add the red wine, and deglaze the pan, using a wooden spoon to scrape up any browned bits. Continue to cook, stirring frequently, until the wine has been absorbed and the onion is golden brown, about 10 minutes. Remove the pan from the heat and transfer the onion to a small bowl.

4. Meanwhile, in a food processor or blender, combine the feta and heavy cream and process until smooth and fully combined, about 30 seconds.

5. Remove the tart shell from the freezer and set the pan on the prepared sheet pan. Spread the feta mixture evenly across the bottom of the shell. Scatter the caramelized onion evenly on top of the feta. Arrange the cherry tomatoes, cut-side up, on top of the onion, alternating colors and pressing them gently into the onion. Sprinkle with the thyme, salt, and pepper.

6. Bake until browned around the edges, about 30 minutes.

7. Let the tart cool for 30 minutes, then slice and serve.

PISSALADIÈRE

serves 6-8

....

This savory tart with a pizza-like crust comes from Nice, in the South of France, where Ben's family often spent summer vacations. If you love the briny flavor of anchovies, traditional in this dish, feel free to add them. The butter adds creaminess, but to make this dish vegan, you can replace it with olive oil. Pissaladière can be served warm or at room temperature and makes a lovely first course, or it can be cut into small pieces for hors d'oeuvres.

DOUGH

1¼ teaspoons active dry yeast

½ teaspoon sugar

1 cup (*240 ml*) warm water (about 100°F / *38°C*)

2¾ cups (*400 g*) bread flour

1 tablespoon fine sea salt

2 tablespoons extra-virgin olive oil, plus more for drizzling

ONION TOPPING

¼ cup (*60 ml*) extra-virgin olive oil

3 yellow onions (about 2 pounds / *900 g*), thinly sliced

2 teaspoons sugar

2 teaspoons fine sea salt

4 tablespoons (2 ounces / *57 g*) unsalted butter

¼ cup (*7 g*) packed fresh rosemary needles, chopped

¼ cup (*7 g*) packed fresh thyme leaves

FINISHING AND ASSEMBLY

3 tablespoons cornmeal

¼ cup (*60 ml*) plus 3 tablespoons (*45 ml*) extra-virgin olive oil

1½ cups (*175 g*) pitted Kalamata or other black olives, halved

Fresh rosemary and thyme sprigs, for garnish

1. MAKE THE DOUGH: Place the yeast and sugar in a stand mixer fitted with the paddle attachment. Add the warm water and let sit for about 10 minutes, or until foamy. (If the yeast doesn't foam up, it's not activated; you'll need to start over with yeast from a new package.)

2. With the mixer running on low, gradually add the flour, followed by the salt, and mix until a shaggy dough forms. Switch to the dough hook attachment, add the 2 tablespoons olive oil, and knead on medium for about 10 minutes, or until the dough is smooth and very soft. Drizzle some olive oil around the sides of the bowl to prevent the dough from sticking, then cover the bowl with a clean kitchen towel and let it sit in a warm place for about 2 hours, or until doubled in size.

3. MEANWHILE, MAKE THE ONION TOPPING: Heat the olive oil in a large nonstick skillet over medium heat. When the oil is shimmering, add the onions and cook, stirring frequently, until soft and translucent, about 10 minutes. Add the sugar and salt and cook, stirring frequently, for about 1 minute. Reduce the heat to medium-low and add a few tablespoons of water to deglaze the pan, using a wooden spoon to scrape up any browned bits off the bottom. Continue to cook, stirring frequently, until all the water is absorbed and the onions are golden brown, about 10 minutes. Add the butter, rosemary, and thyme and stir until the butter is melted and coats the onions. Transfer the mixture to a medium bowl.

4. FINISH THE CRUST: Sprinkle a 17¼ × 12¼-inch (*43 cm × 30.5 cm*) or similarly sized sheet pan with the cornmeal.

5. When the dough has doubled in size, gently punch it down in the center. Turn out the dough onto the cornmeal-dusted sheet pan, then knead and stretch the dough to reach the edges of the pan.

Brush the dough with 3 tablespoons of the olive oil, cover with a clean kitchen towel, and let sit in a warm place until puffed, about 1½ hours.

6. Preheat the oven to 425°F (*218°C*).

7. **ASSEMBLE THE TART:** Spread the onion topping evenly across the surface of the dough, leaving a ¼-inch (*5 mm*) border. Sprinkle the olives on top and drizzle with the remaining ¼ cup (*60 ml*) of olive oil.

8. Transfer to the oven and bake until the crust is browned on the bottom and sides, about 20 minutes. Let rest for 10 minutes, then cut, garnish with rosemary and thyme, and enjoy immediately or at room temperature.

sandwiches and tartines

"My favorite memories of cooking with my maman all involve something going horribly wrong—from forgetting beef tenderloin in the oven to disturbingly clumpy Thanksgiving gravy. She never took anything in the kitchen too seriously, kept us all laughing, and rectified every culinary mishap with a perfect grilled cheese."

—SERENA WOLF,
chef and author, *The Dude Diet*

CROQUE-MAMAN

makes 2 sandwiches

....

The earliest recorded appearance of a croque-monsieur was on a Paris café menu in 1910, while its first literary reference came in 1918, in volume two of Marcel Proust's *In Search of Lost Time*. A go-to snack in Paris cafés and bars, this hot ham and cheese sandwich is a staple of the maman lunch menu. If you add a fried egg, it becomes a croque-madame, which makes for a hearty breakfast. Ours, renamed croque-maman, is pretty traditional, but we also serve a variation with truffle béchamel—you can achieve a similar effect with shaved truffles or truffle oil.

BÉCHAMEL

1⅓ cups (*315 ml*) whole milk

2 tablespoons unsalted butter

¼ cup (*36 g*) all-purpose flour

½ teaspoon grated nutmeg

½ teaspoon freshly ground black pepper

¼ teaspoon fine sea salt

CROQUE-MAMANS

4 slices brioche or challah, about ½ inch (*1.25 cm*) thick

½ teaspoon Dijon mustard

2 slices Parisian ham (jambon de Paris; see Tip) or slow-cooked deli ham

⅔ cup (*80 g*) grated Comté or Gruyère cheese

notes

....

....

....

....

....

....

1. MAKE THE BÉCHAMEL: In a small saucepan, warm the milk over medium heat until hot but not simmering, keeping a close eye to make sure the milk doesn't boil over.

2. Meanwhile, melt the butter in a separate small saucepan over low heat. Add the flour and cook, stirring with a wooden spoon, until the butter mixture is bubbling but hasn't started to brown, about 2 minutes. Slowly add the hot milk to the butter and flour and cook, whisking constantly, until smooth, about 2 minutes. Remove the pan from the heat and stir in the nutmeg, pepper, and salt.

3. Set a rack 2 to 4 inches (*5 to 10 cm*) from the oven's heat source and turn the broiler to high.

4. ASSEMBLE THE CROQUE-MAMANS: Using a toaster or the oven, toast the bread just until very light brown. Transfer the bread to a sheet pan. Using a pastry brush, brush a thin layer of mustard on 2 slices, then top each with a slice of ham. Sprinkle most of the Comté over the ham. Spread a thin layer of béchamel on the other 2 slices of bread and arrange them on top of the Comté to close the sandwiches. Spread the remaining béchamel sauce generously on top of the sandwiches and sprinkle the remaining Comté on top. Broil for 2 to 4 minutes, rotating the sheet pan as needed for even toasting, until the topping is melted, bubbling, and lightly browned. Serve hot.

TIP: *Not all hams are created equal, so it's best to head to the butcher to get the good stuff. Parisian ham, or jambon de Paris, is slow-cooked rather than smoked, which makes for juicier, more flavorful meat, perfect for bistro-style classics like this croque-maman or Quiche Lorraine with Parisian Ham and Comté (page 84).*

JANICE TARTINE
EGG SALAD WITH AVOCADO, WATERMELON RADISH, PICKLES, AND SPROUTS

makes 4 tartines

....

Egg salad was a lunchtime staple when Elisa was growing up and a dish she made with both her maman, Janice, and her grandmother. Elisa's job was to peel the eggs, which is how she figured out that it's easier to do when you keep them submerged in ice water. The egg salad's secret ingredient is cornichon juice, which has helped make this sandwich a hit at maman since day one—regular dill pickles can be used in place of the cornichons. To lighten the salad, you can swap in Greek yogurt for the mayo, but don't skip the avocado or radishes, as they add color, flavor, and texture.

8 large eggs

1 large celery stalk (about 2½ ounces / *70 g*), thinly sliced

¼ large red onion (about 2 ounces / *57 g*), finely chopped

⅓ cup (*50 g*) finely chopped French cornichons, plus 1 tablespoon strained cornichon juice

3 tablespoons mayonnaise

1 tablespoon Dijon mustard

2 tablespoons finely chopped fresh dill

1 tablespoon fresh flat-leaf parsley leaves, thinly sliced

Fine sea salt and freshly ground black pepper

4 large slices country bread

2 avocados (about 5½ ounces / *154 g* each), sliced

4 watermelon radishes (about 2 ounces / *57 g* each), thinly sliced

Small handful of microgreens or sunflower sprouts

notes

_____

_____

_____

_____

1. Place the eggs in a large saucepan and add enough cold water to cover by ½ inch (*1.25 cm*). Bring to a boil, then immediately remove the pan from the heat, cover, and let stand for 10 minutes. Meanwhile, fill a large bowl with ice water. After 10 minutes, use a slotted spoon to transfer the eggs to the ice water and let stand for 5 minutes. With the eggs still submerged in the ice water or while holding them under cold running water, peel and discard the shells.

2. Roughly chop the eggs and transfer to a medium bowl. Add the celery, red onion, cornichons, cornichon juice, mayonnaise, mustard, dill, and parsley and gently fold to combine. Season to taste with salt and pepper, cover, and refrigerate until ready to use or for up to 3 days.

3. Using a toaster or the oven, toast the bread just until very light brown.

4. Spread the egg salad evenly on the toasted bread, being sure to cover the entire surface and pressing lightly to pack it together. Top the tartines with the avocado, watermelon radish, and microgreens. Cut in half and serve.

GINA SANDWICH
HERBED TUNA SALAD WITH OLIVE-CAPER GREMOLATA
makes 3 sandwiches

....

Our former head chef Tawni created this dressed-up tuna salad sandwich in honor of the sandwiches her maman, Gina, used to make for her. She took inspiration from France's salade Niçoise, which is why the tuna is paired with our olive-caper gremolata.

1 cup (*200 g*) cherry tomatoes, halved

2 teaspoons extra-virgin olive oil

Fine sea salt

3 (5-ounce / *140 g*) cans wild-caught tuna in olive oil, drained

6 tablespoons (*70 g*) mayonnaise

½ cup (*13 g*) packed chopped fresh dill

4 scallions, sliced

1 tablespoon dried tarragon

½ teaspoon freshly ground black pepper

1 (25-inch / *63 cm*) baguette

¾ cup (*170 g*) Olive-Caper Gremolata (page 64)

1. Preheat the oven to 350°F (*180°C*). Line a sheet pan with parchment paper.

2. In a medium bowl, toss the cherry tomatoes with the olive oil and ¼ teaspoon salt. Spread in an even layer on the prepared sheet pan and roast until soft and lightly browned at the edges, about 25 minutes. Transfer to a medium bowl and refrigerate until ready to use.

3. In another medium bowl, combine the tuna, mayonnaise, dill, scallions, tarragon, pepper, and 1 teaspoon salt and stir until fully incorporated. Add the cherry tomatoes, along with any juices they released, and gently fold to incorporate. Season with more salt to taste, cover, and refrigerate until ready to use.

4. Cut the baguette into thirds, then slice each piece horizontally in half. Using a toaster or the oven, toast just until very light brown.

5. Spread tuna salad on each of the bottom halves of the baguette, pressing lightly to pack it together. Spread some gremolata on the top halves, being sure it covers the entire surface of the bread. Close the sandwiches, halve diagonally, and serve.

notes

....
....
....
....
....
....

SOPHIE SANDWICH
CURRIED CAULIFLOWER WITH PICKLED CUCUMBERS, POMEGRANATE, AND MINT YOGURT

makes 4 sandwiches

This unusual sandwich, named in honor of Elisa's great-aunt Sophie, features one of our favorite ingredients: cauliflower. We flavor this versatile veggie with curry and combine it with chickpeas, raisins, and pomegranate seeds, then pile it on ciabatta rolls with mint yogurt and pickled cucumbers. These sandwiches can be served cold or at room temperature; make them vegan with dairy-free yogurt.

CURRIED CAULIFLOWER SALAD

1 large head cauliflower (about 2 pounds 3 ounces / *1 kg*), cut into small florets

½ cup (*120 ml*) extra-virgin olive oil

1 garlic clove, minced

6 teaspoons curry powder

2 teaspoons ground turmeric

Fine sea salt and freshly ground black pepper

1 (15.5-ounce / *439 g*) can chickpeas, drained and rinsed

¾ cup (*110 g*) raisins

1 cup (*140 g*) pomegranate seeds

2 tablespoons fresh lemon juice

MINT YOGURT

¾ cup plus 2 tablespoons (*210 g*) plain Greek yogurt

7 large fresh mint leaves, thinly sliced

¼ teaspoon ground cumin

Fine sea salt and freshly ground black pepper

SANDWICHES

4 (5½-inch / *14 cm*) ciabatta rolls

1 cup (*200 g*) pickled cucumbers, homemade (see Pickled Vegetables, page 104) or store-bought

1. Preheat the oven to 400°F (*200°C*). Line two sheet pans with parchment paper.

2. **MAKE THE CURRIED CAULIFLOWER SALAD:** In a medium bowl, toss the cauliflower with 2 tablespoons of the olive oil, the garlic, 5 teaspoons of the curry powder, 1½ teaspoons of the turmeric, 1 teaspoon salt, and ¼ teaspoon pepper. Spread in an even layer on one of the prepared sheet pans. Transfer to the oven and roast until lightly browned and easily pierced with a fork, about 20 minutes. Let cool slightly before using.

3. Meanwhile, in a small bowl, toss the chickpeas with 2 tablespoons of the olive oil and the remaining 1 teaspoon curry powder and ½ teaspoon turmeric. Spread in an even layer on the other prepared sheet pan and roast alongside the cauliflower until sizzling, about 8 minutes. Let cool slightly.

4. Bring a small pot of water to a boil over high heat. Add the raisins, then remove the pot from the heat and let stand for 15 minutes to plump the raisins. Drain the raisins and discard the water.

5. In a food processor, combine the cauliflower and chickpeas and pulse for about 1 minute, or until a chunky puree forms. Transfer to a large bowl and add the rehydrated raisins, pomegranate seeds, lemon juice, 2 teaspoons salt, and the remaining ¼ cup (*60 ml*) olive oil. Stir to combine. Season to taste with salt. Refrigerate until ready to use.

6. **MAKE THE MINT YOGURT:** In a small bowl, combine the yogurt, mint, and cumin and stir to combine. Season to taste with salt and pepper.

7. **MAKE THE SANDWICHES:** Slice the ciabatta rolls in half horizontally. Using a toaster or the oven, toast just until very light brown.

8. Tightly pack the curried cauliflower salad onto the bottom of each roll, then top each with some of the pickled cucumbers. Spread some of the mint yogurt on each of the roll tops, then arrange them on top of the pickled cucumbers to close the sandwiches. Cut each sandwich in half and serve.

JESSALYN SANDWICH
HALLOUMI WITH EGGPLANT, CUCUMBERS, AND PICKLED RED ONIONS

makes 3 sandwiches

....

Halloumi is a springy cheese with a mild, tangy flavor and a pronounced saltiness. Unlike most other cheeses, Halloumi doesn't melt; rather, it simply browns and crisps, creating a unique and irresistible texture. In this sandwich, named for a dear friend of maman, we pair it with a tahini-infused eggplant spread, crisp cucumbers, and pickled red onions. It's wonderfully colorful and a true bite of summer. Vegans can swap sliced avocado for the cheese.

EGGPLANT SPREAD

1 medium eggplant (about 15 ounces / *420 g*)

2 tablespoons extra-virgin olive oil

½ cup (*13 g*) packed fresh flat-leaf parsley leaves

1 garlic clove, peeled

2 tablespoons tahini

1 tablespoon fresh lemon juice

¾ teaspoon paprika

¾ teaspoon fine sea salt

SANDWICHES

1 (25-inch / *63 cm*) baguette

1 tablespoon extra-virgin olive oil

12 ounces (*340 g*) Halloumi cheese, sliced ¼ inch (*5 mm*) thick

1 medium cucumber (about 10 ounces / *280 g*), sliced

3 or 4 fresh mint sprigs

½ cup (50 g) pickled red onions, homemade (see Pickled Vegetables, recipe follows) or store-bought

1. MAKE THE EGGPLANT SPREAD: Preheat the oven to 350°F (*180°C*). Line a sheet pan with parchment paper.

2. Cut off and discard the ends of the eggplant and halve the eggplant lengthwise. Arrange, cut-side up, on the parchment-lined sheet pan. Use a small knife to stab the flesh of the eggplant a few times, then drizzle 1 tablespoon olive oil over each eggplant half and use clean hands to rub it into the flesh. Bake until dark brown and very tender, about 40 minutes. Let cool slightly and then scrape the flesh out of the eggplant and discard the skin.

3. In a food processor, combine the parsley and garlic and process for about 1 minute to very finely chop. Add the eggplant, tahini, lemon juice, paprika, and salt. Blend for about 30 seconds, then scrape down the sides of the bowl and process until very smooth, 1 to 2 minutes more. Transfer to an airtight container and refrigerate until ready to use or for up to 4 days.

4. MAKE THE SANDWICHES: Cut the baguette into thirds and then cut each piece horizontally in half. Using a toaster or the oven, toast just until very light brown.

5. Divide the eggplant spread evenly among the tops and bottoms of the baguette pieces.

RECIPE CONTINUES

6. Heat the olive oil in a nonstick medium skillet over high heat. When the oil is shimmering, wait another minute to be sure it is very hot. Reduce the heat to medium, add the Halloumi, and cook until golden brown on both sides, about 1 minute per side. Divide the Halloumi among the bottom halves of the sandwiches. Layer the sandwiches with the cucumber slices, mint leaves, and pickled onions. Finish the sandwiches with the tops, halve diagonally, and serve.

PICKLED VEGETABLES

MAKES 8 CUPS (*1.9 liters*)

8 cups thinly sliced vegetables, such as 3 red onions (about 2 pounds / *900 g*) or 2 large cucumbers (1¾ pounds / *800 g*)

4 cups (*960 ml*) white wine vinegar or distilled white vinegar

¼ cup (*50 g*) sugar

¼ cup (*62 g*) fine sea salt

1. Place the vegetables in a 4-quart (*3.8 liter*) glass jar or other airtight heatproof container.

2. In a large pot, combine the vinegar, 4 cups (*960 ml*) water, the sugar, and salt and bring to a boil over high heat, stirring occasionally to dissolve the sugar and salt.

3. Carefully pour the hot liquid over the vegetables. Use a wooden spoon to push the vegetables down, being sure they are completely submerged. Let stand at room temperature for about 1 hour, or until no longer steaming. Seal the jar and refrigerate for at least 24 hours before using. Store the pickled vegetables refrigerated for up to 1 month.

notes

ANNABEL SANDWICH
CAULIFLOWER GRILLED CHEESE
WITH ROMESCO DIPPING SAUCE

makes 4 sandwiches

With cauliflower, Cheddar, goat cheese, and an irresistible dipping sauce, this sandwich—named for one of our servers—is a sophisticated take on the classic grilled cheese and tomato soup combo. We find kids don't notice the cauliflower, while adults go mad for the romesco, a rich tomato-based sauce that's thickened with bread and nuts. Romesco can also be made in a food processor, but it might take a few extra minutes to create a smooth sauce.

ROMESCO SAUCE

2 end slices stale country bread (about 1½ ounces / *42 g*), torn

3 vine-ripened tomatoes (about 13½ ounces / *378 g*), cored and each cut into 8 pieces

3 garlic cloves, peeled

6 tablespoons (*42 g*) sliced raw unsalted almonds

1 tablespoon extra-virgin olive oil

2 cups (*440 g*) jarred roasted red peppers

3 tablespoons red wine vinegar

1 tablespoon paprika

1½ teaspoons fine sea salt

¼ teaspoon cayenne pepper

SANDWICHES

1 head cauliflower (about 1½ pounds / *675 g*), cut into florets

¼ cup (*60 ml*) extra-virgin olive oil

2 teaspoons fine sea salt

½ teaspoon freshly ground black pepper

8 large slices country bread

12 slices sharp white Cheddar cheese (about 8 ounces / *225 g*)

3 ounces (*84 g*) crumbled goat cheese

¼ cup (*7 g*) packed fresh dill

1. MAKE THE ROMESCO SAUCE: Preheat the oven to 400°F (*200°C*). Line a sheet pan with parchment paper.

2. Spread the bread in an even layer on the prepared sheet pan. Bake until browned and crunchy, about 5 minutes. Transfer to a small bowl and let cool. Leave the oven on; reserve the parchment-lined sheet pan.

3. In a medium bowl, toss the tomatoes with the garlic, almonds, and olive oil. Spread in an even layer on the reserved sheet pan and roast until the tomatoes are soft and the almonds are deep brown, 10 to 12 minutes. Transfer to a medium bowl and let cool for about 5 minutes. Reserve the sheet pan and leave the oven on; discard the parchment paper.

4. In a blender, combine the bread, roasted red peppers, vinegar, paprika, salt, and cayenne. Gradually turn the blender to high and let run until the bread is chopped, about 30 seconds. Add the cooled tomato mixture and blend on high, scraping the blender as needed, until completely smooth, 1 to 2 minutes. Refrigerate until ready to use.

5. MAKE THE SANDWICHES: Line the reserved sheet pan with clean parchment paper.

6. In a medium bowl, toss the cauliflower with 2 tablespoons of the olive oil, the salt, and pepper. Spread in an even layer on the prepared sheet pan and roast until lightly browned and easily pierced with a fork, about 20 minutes. Let cool slightly.

7. Place 4 slices of bread on a cutting board and top each with 2 slices of Cheddar. Divide the roasted

RECIPE CONTINUES

cauliflower and goat cheese evenly among the sandwiches and sprinkle each with dill. Top with the remaining 4 slices of Cheddar and then with the remaining 4 slices of bread to close the sandwiches.

8. Heat 1 tablespoon of the olive oil in a large nonstick skillet over medium heat. When the oil is shimmering, wait another minute to be sure it is very hot. Add 2 sandwiches to the skillet, reduce the heat to medium-low, cover, and cook until the bottom slices are deep golden brown, about 3 minutes. Flip the sandwiches over, cover again, and cook until the cheese is fully melted and both slices of bread are deep golden brown, about 3 minutes more. Repeat to cook the remaining 2 sandwiches, using the remaining 1 tablespoon olive oil. Let the sandwiches rest for 1 minute, then cut diagonally in half and serve with the romesco sauce alongside for dipping.

TIP: *Store the romesco refrigerated in an airtight container for up to 5 days.*

notes

CLAUDIA SANDWICH

BALSAMIC MUSHROOMS WITH CALABRIAN CHILE–FETA SPREAD, BASIL PESTO, AND ARUGULA

makes 3 sandwiches

....

With roasted balsamic mushrooms, a spicy feta spread, and pesto, this sandwich—named for the maman of a former employee who is still part of the maman family—requires a bit of effort, but you won't regret it. Plus, both the mushrooms and feta spread can be prepped in advance, and you can save time by using store-bought pesto. Look for Calabrian chiles in specialty or Italian markets or substitute any jarred hot peppers packed in oil. We serve this sandwich warm at maman, but it's just as good at room temperature.

CALABRIAN CHILE–FETA SPREAD

¼ cup (*45 g*) drained oil-packed Calabrian chiles, stems removed

¼ cup (*6 g*) packed fresh flat-leaf parsley leaves

1 garlic clove, peeled

7 ounces (*200 g*) cream cheese, at room temperature, cut into small chunks

½ teaspoon fresh lemon juice

¼ teaspoon fine sea salt

1⅓ cups (*150 g*) crumbled feta cheese

SANDWICHES

5 large portobello mushrooms (about 1¼ pounds / *560 g*), stems discarded and caps cut into strips ½ inch (*1.25 cm*) wide

1 cup (*240 ml*) Balsamic Vinaigrette (page 125) or store-bought

1 (25-inch / *63 cm*) baguette

½ cup (*100 g*) Basil Pesto (page 127) or store-bought

¾ cup (*30 g*) packed baby arugula

1. MAKE THE CALABRIAN CHILE–FETA SPREAD: In a food processor, combine the Calabrian chiles, parsley, and garlic and process until finely chopped, about 30 seconds. Add the cream cheese, lemon juice, and salt and process until very smooth, about 1 minute. Add the feta and blend until the cheeses are combined and the spread is mostly smooth, about 30 seconds. Refrigerate until ready to use.

2. MAKE THE SANDWICHES: Preheat the oven to 400°F (*200°C*). Line a sheet pan with parchment paper.

3. In a large bowl, toss the portobello mushrooms with the vinaigrette. Spread the mushrooms in an even layer on the prepared sheet pan and roast until the mushrooms have soaked up most of the vinaigrette and are browned around the edges, about 15 minutes. Transfer the mushrooms to a large bowl. Leave the oven on. Reserve the sheet pan and line it with new parchment paper.

4. Cut the baguette into thirds and then halve each piece horizontally. Divide the feta spread evenly among the bottom halves of the baguette and spread the pesto on the top halves. Divide the mushrooms among the bottom halves. Arrange on the prepared sheet pan and toast until the edges of the bread are crisp and the spreads are warm, 4 to 5 minutes. Arrange a little arugula on top of the mushrooms, then finish the sandwiches with the tops. Halve diagonally and serve.

TIP: *Store the Calabrian chile-feta spread in the refrigerator in an airtight container for up to 5 days.*

KATIE SANDWICH

ROASTED CHICKEN WITH TOMATO, ROASTED RED PEPPERS, ARUGULA, AND BASIL AÏOLI

makes 3 sandwiches

Rotisserie chicken is a favorite in our extended family—Ben remembers cooking poulet roti with his dad, and Elisa's father loves to barbecue—so we're always looking for creative ways to transform the leftovers, like this sandwich that layers cooked chicken breast with roasted cherry tomatoes, roasted red peppers, arugula, and basil aïoli. It can be made with rotisserie, roasted, or even poached chicken. Named for a former maman chef, it's one of the most beloved sandwiches at maman. You can make it vegetarian by swapping the chicken for grilled Halloumi—it's just as good.

BASIL AÏOLI

2⅔ cups (*80 g*) packed fresh basil leaves

1 cup (*187 g*) mayonnaise

1 tablespoon Dijon mustard

SANDWICHES

1¾ cups (*350 g*) cherry tomatoes

1 tablespoon extra-virgin olive oil

Fine sea salt and freshly ground black pepper

1 (25-inch / *63 cm*) baguette

¾ cup (*165 g*) jarred roasted red peppers

12 to 15 ounces (*340 to 420 g*) cooked boneless, skinless chicken breast, thickly sliced

¾ cup (*30 g*) packed baby arugula

1. **MAKE THE BASIL AÏOLI:** In a food processor, process the basil until finely chopped, 2 to 3 minutes. Add the mayonnaise and mustard and blend until the mixture is light green and the basil is very finely chopped, about 1 minute.

2. **MAKE THE SANDWICHES:** Preheat the oven to 350°F (*180°C*). Line a sheet pan with parchment paper.

3. In a medium bowl, toss the cherry tomatoes with the olive oil and season with salt and pepper. Spread in an even layer on the prepared sheet pan and bake until very soft, 25 to 30 minutes. Transfer to a medium bowl and let cool. Increase the oven temperature to 400°F (*200°C*). Reserve the sheet pan and line it with new parchment paper.

4. Cut the baguette into thirds, then slice each piece horizontally in half. Spread the basil aïoli on the baguette halves, then divide the roasted red peppers and chicken among the bottom halves. Arrange the top and bottom halves of the baguette on the prepared sheet pan and toast until the edges of the bread are crisp and the chicken is warm, about 3 minutes. Arrange a few slices of roasted tomato and a little arugula on top of the chicken, then close the sandwiches. Halve diagonally and serve.

notes

DELICATA SQUASH, TALEGGIO, ARUGULA, AND HAZELNUT FOCACCIA

serves 4

Airy focaccia is topped with sweet delicata squash, aromatic Taleggio, bitter arugula, and crunchy hazelnuts to create this autumn tartine. Delicata squash has pale yellow skin with green striations and a lovely scalloped shape, so it looks particularly pretty cut into rings for this tartine. And it doesn't require peeling, so it's practically fuss-free!

1 large delicata squash (about 1 pound 2 ounces / *500 g*), seeded and cut crosswise into rings ¼ inch (*5 mm*) thick

3 tablespoons maple syrup

¼ cup plus 1 tablespoon (*75 ml*) extra-virgin olive oil

1¼ teaspoons fine sea salt

1 cup (*25 g*) packed fresh flat-leaf parsley leaves, finely chopped

½ cup (*68 g*) skinned hazelnuts, roughly chopped

1 (12 × 9-inch / *30 × 23 cm*) piece focaccia

9 ounces (*252 g*) Taleggio cheese, cut into thin slices

2 cups (*88 g*) packed baby arugula

1. Preheat the oven to 350°F (*180°C*). Line a sheet pan with parchment paper.

2. In a large bowl, toss the squash with the maple syrup, 1 tablespoon of the olive oil, and 1 teaspoon of the salt. Spread in an even layer on the prepared sheet pan and bake until tender and easily pierced with a fork, about 20 minutes. Set aside to cool and increase the oven temperature to 400°F (*200°C*).

3. In a small bowl, stir together the parsley, hazelnuts, and the remaining ¼ cup (*60 ml*) olive oil and ¼ teaspoon salt.

4. Set the focaccia on a sheet pan. Spread the parsley-hazelnut mixture in an even layer across the entire surface. Arrange the squash rings on top, overlapping them to cover the focaccia evenly. Spread the Taleggio slices evenly across the focaccia and bake until the cheese is completely melted and the focaccia has crisped, about 10 minutes.

5. Transfer to a wire rack and let rest for 10 minutes. Cut the focaccia into 4 large squares, then halve each square diagonally. Top with the baby arugula and serve warm.

notes

BIBIANE SANDWICH

TURKEY WITH PICKLED ONIONS, CHEDDAR, AND A KALE, PEA, AND RICOTTA SPREAD

makes 4 sandwiches

....

Bibiane is the maman of our former events director, Hortense Catteau, but we've all embraced her as our own French maman. Whether visiting New York or at her home in France, Bibiane always found ways to help and support us—from cooking for the staff to sending recipe inspiration to sewing our linens. We serve the Bibiane as a full-size sandwich at maman, but it's also lovely cut into squares for a tea party spread. You'll have a little bit extra of the kale, pea, and ricotta spread, but this is a very good thing. It can be stored in an airtight container and refrigerated for several days and is great on other sandwiches.

KALE, PEA, AND RICOTTA SPREAD

2 cups (*80 g*) packed baby kale leaves

1 garlic clove, peeled

1½ cups (*338 g*) whole-milk ricotta cheese

2 teaspoons fresh lemon juice

1 teaspoon fine sea salt

¼ teaspoon freshly ground black pepper

¼ teaspoon grated nutmeg

⅛ teaspoon crushed red pepper flakes

¾ cup (*100 g*) frozen peas, thawed

SANDWICHES

8 large slices country bread

8 slices sharp white Cheddar cheese (about 5½ ounces / *154 g*)

½ cup (*50 g*) pickled onions (see Pickled Vegetables, page 104)

12 thin slices roast turkey breast

2 tablespoons extra-virgin olive oil

notes

1. **MAKE THE KALE, PEA, AND RICOTTA SPREAD:** In a food processor, combine the kale and garlic and process until very finely chopped, about 1 minute. Transfer to a small bowl.

2. In the food processor, combine the ricotta, lemon juice, salt, pepper, nutmeg, and pepper flakes and process until very smooth, about 30 seconds. Scrape down the sides of the bowl, then add the chopped kale mixture and the peas and pulse about 5 times, until the ingredients are well mixed and the spread is mostly smooth.

3. **MAKE THE SANDWICHES:** Place 4 slices of bread on a cutting board and layer each with 2 slices of Cheddar, some pickled onions, and 3 slices of roast turkey breast. Spread some kale, pea, and ricotta spread on each of the remaining 4 slices of bread and close up the sandwiches.

4. Heat 1 tablespoon of the olive oil in a large nonstick skillet over medium heat. When the oil is shimmering, wait another minute to be sure it is very hot. Add 2 sandwiches to the skillet, reduce the heat to medium-low, cover, and cook until the bottom slice is deep golden brown, about 2 minutes. Flip the sandwiches over, cover, and cook until the cheese is melted and both slices of bread are deep golden brown, about 3 minutes more. Repeat to cook the remaining 2 sandwiches, using the remaining 1 tablespoon of olive oil. Let the sandwiches rest for 1 minute, then halve diagonally and serve.

salads and soups

"Whether teaching kids how to cook in classes at my studio or teaching my own children at home, I believe in learning through interactive fun, and I hope to pass along my culinary curiosity, adventurous palate, and love of eating."

—Cricket Azima,
founder of the Creative Kitchen + Kids Food Festival

PHYLLIS SALAD
APPLE AND CASHEW SPINACH SALAD
WITH CURRY VINAIGRETTE

serves 2-4

Andrea, our marketing director, inherited this recipe from her maman, Phyllis. It really shines in the fall, especially when made with local apples, but Andrea's family asks Phyllis to make it year-round, every time they gather together. And Andrea brings it to all our staff potlucks—everyone loves the unique curry vinaigrette, and the salad is vegan, so no one is ever left out.

CURRY VINAIGRETTE

2 tablespoons Dijon mustard

2 tablespoons white wine vinegar

1 tablespoon dry white wine (see Tip)

1 teaspoon soy sauce

2 tablespoons sugar

1 teaspoon curry powder

½ teaspoon fine sea salt

¼ teaspoon freshly ground black pepper

½ cup (*120 ml*) extra-virgin olive oil

SALAD

¾ cup (*105 g*) raw unsalted cashews, chopped

2 tablespoons sesame seeds

5 cups (*125 g*) packed baby spinach

1 Granny Smith apple (about 3 ounces / *84 g*), very thinly sliced

4 scallions, sliced

¼ cup (*40 g*) dried cranberries

notes

1. Preheat the oven to 400°F (*200°C*).

2. **MAKE THE CURRY VINAIGRETTE:** In a small bowl, whisk together the mustard, vinegar, wine, and soy sauce. Add the sugar, curry powder, salt, and pepper and whisk until the sugar is dissolved. While whisking, slowly drizzle in the olive oil, then continue whisking until fully emulsified.

3. **MAKE THE SALAD:** Spread the cashews evenly in a small ovenproof skillet and toast in the oven until golden brown and fragrant, about 10 minutes. Transfer the cashews to a small bowl and let cool. Spread the sesame seeds evenly in the same small skillet and toast in the oven until golden brown and fragrant, about 5 minutes. Transfer the sesame seeds to another small bowl and let cool.

4. In a large bowl, toss together the spinach, apple, scallions, cranberries, and cashews.

5. Drizzle the curry vinaigrette over the salad and toss to coat. Divide among four bowls, sprinkle each with the toasted sesame seeds, and serve.

TIP: *If you don't have dry white wine on hand, use an additional tablespoon of white wine vinegar.*

TOMATO BREAD SALAD

serves 4

....

Our take on panzanella combines our culinary backgrounds. Ben has Italian roots on his father's side and Italian is his favorite cuisine, but to give this salad some Canadian flair, we add Montreal steak seasoning, which is Elisa's maman's go-to seasoning for everything from chicken to fries to macaroni and cheese. Panzanella is often made with stale bread, but we find toasting fresh bread creates a better texture. Using flavor-packed cherry tomatoes means you can enjoy this salad year-round, but in summer, when tomatoes are ripe and beautiful, use whatever variety looks best.

5 cups cubed ciabatta or rustic sourdough bread (about 11 ounces / *310 g*)

½ cup (*120 ml*) extra-virgin olive oil (see Tips)

2 teaspoons Montreal steak seasoning

2 pounds (*900 g*) cherry or grape tomatoes, halved

1 small shallot, shaved or thinly sliced

¼ cup (*6 g*) packed fresh flat-leaf parsley leaves, finely chopped

3 tablespoons white wine vinegar

1 garlic clove, minced

1. Preheat the oven to 350°F (*180°C*). Line a sheet pan with parchment paper.

2. In a large bowl, combine the bread with ¼ cup (*60 ml*) of the olive oil and the steak seasoning and toss to coat. Spread in an even layer on the prepared sheet pan and bake until the bread is crisp and firm but not browned, about 15 minutes. Let cool.

3. In the same bowl, combine the tomatoes, shallot, and parsley. Add the cooled bread and toss to combine.

4. In a small bowl, whisk together the remaining ¼ cup (*60 ml*) olive oil, the vinegar, and the garlic. Add to the bread and tomato mixture, toss to coat, and let stand at room temperature, tossing occasionally, until the bread has absorbed most of the dressing, 20 to 30 minutes. Serve immediately.

TIPS:
We always stock two extra-virgin olive oils at home and at our restaurants: a basic one for everyday cooking and baking, and a more luxurious oil for salads and finishing dishes.

All extra-virgin olive oil is made from pure, cold-pressed olives, but we love to use one with grassy, peppery notes to enhance the flavor of dishes like this salad.

notes

....
....
....
....
....
....

MÉMÉ'S COUSCOUS TABOULÉ

serves 4-6

....

Mémé—grandma in French—is Ben's grandmother Fatima, who was originally from Algeria and brought a lot of Mediterranean influence to their family's kitchen in the South of France. Taboulé is traditionally made with bulgur, but we love it with couscous, which doesn't need to be cooked for this recipe. The trick is to combine all the ingredients and refrigerate the salad for about 4 hours, allowing the lemon juice, olive oil, and the natural juice from the veggies to "cook" the grain. If you're in a rush, of course, you can simply cook the couscous or sub in your favorite cooked grain. We like to serve this summery salad alongside any quiche, or top it with grilled chicken or salmon.

1½ cups (*300 g*) couscous (see Tip)

1½ cups (*300 g*) cherry tomatoes, diced or quartered

1 green bell pepper (about 9 ounces / *252 g*), diced

1 large cucumber (about 14 ounces / *400 g*), diced

½ large red onion (about 4½ ounces / *126 g*), diced

½ cup (*120 ml*) extra-virgin olive oil

⅓ cup (*75 ml*) fresh lemon juice

1 cup (*245 g*) plain yogurt

1 cup (*187 g*) mayonnaise

2 teaspoons poppy seeds

½ cup (*10 g*) packed fresh flat-leaf parsley leaves, finely chopped

½ cup (*10 g*) packed fresh mint leaves, finely chopped

Fine sea salt and freshly ground black pepper

1. In a large bowl, combine the couscous, tomatoes, bell pepper, cucumber, onion, olive oil, and lemon juice and toss to combine. Transfer to an airtight container and refrigerate for at least 4 hours or overnight.

2. In a small bowl, whisk together the yogurt, mayonnaise, and poppy seeds.

3. Just before serving, add the parsley and mint to the salad, season to taste with salt and pepper, and stir to incorporate. Divide evenly among four bowls. Drizzle the yogurt sauce over the top without mixing it in or serve it alongside.

TIP: *This salad is just as delicious made with quinoa, orzo, or Israeli couscous. However, you'll need to cook those in advance—only traditional couscous can be "cooked" by soaking in the natural juices of the salad.*

notes

SAUCISSON PASTA SALAD

serves 4

....

This almost effortless pasta salad brings together Ben's three favorite foods: pasta, cheese, and charcuterie. You can use store-bought bread crumbs, but we always recommend making your own—once you see how easy it is and how much better the texture and flavor are, you'll be a believer. This salad keeps quite well and is great cold or at room temperature, so it's wonderful for picnics and packed lunches.

Fine sea salt and freshly ground black pepper

1 pound (*450 g*) fusilli pasta

3 slices stale country or sourdough bread, torn

4 large leeks (about 2½ pounds / *1.1 kg*), cut into rings and well washed (see Tip, page 67)

⅔ cup (*150 ml*) extra-virgin olive oil

7 ounces (*200 g*) saucisson sec or Italian dry-cured salami

2 cups (*88 g*) packed mesclun or baby arugula

1 cup (*95 g*) shredded Asiago cheese

Balsamic Vinaigrette (recipe follows)

1. Preheat the oven to 400°F (*200°C*). Line a sheet pan with parchment paper.

2. Bring a large pot of generously salted water to a boil. Add the fusilli and cook according to the package directions, until al dente, about 8 minutes. Drain in a colander, then rinse with cold water to cool the pasta and stop the cooking process. Shake well to remove any excess water, then transfer to a large bowl.

3. Meanwhile, spread the torn bread in an even layer on the prepared sheet pan. Bake until thoroughly toasted and browned, 5 to 8 minutes. Transfer to a food processor and let cool slightly; reserve the parchment-lined sheet pan. Process until chopped into small chunks and tiny crumbs, about 1 minute. Measure out ¾ cup (*75 g*) of the bread crumbs and reserve the rest for another use.

4. In a medium bowl, toss the leeks with ⅓ cup (*75 ml*) of the olive oil and a pinch of salt. Spread in an even layer on the reserved parchment-lined sheet pan and roast until the edges are browned and a little crispy, 15 to 20 minutes. Add to the pasta.

5. Remove and discard the casings from the saucisson sec. Halve lengthwise, then cut crosswise into half-moons. Add to the leeks and pasta, along with the mesclun and Asiago, and toss to combine. Drizzle in the remaining ⅓ cup (*75 ml*) olive oil and season to taste with salt and pepper. Add the bread crumbs and stir to incorporate.

6. Divide evenly among four bowls and serve with the vinaigrette on the side.

notes

_____

_____

_____

_____

_____

BALSAMIC VINAIGRETTE

MAKES 4 CUPS (*960 ml*)

1 cup (*240 ml*) balsamic vinegar

1 cup (*250 g*) Dijon mustard

¾ cup (*180 ml*) honey

1¼ cups (*300 ml*) extra-virgin olive oil

In a blender, combine the vinegar, mustard, and honey and blend on medium for about 10 seconds, then increase the speed to medium-high and slowly drizzle in the olive oil, blending until fully emulsified. Store refrigerated in an airtight container for up to 2 weeks.

ZUCCHINI, AVOCADO, AND PESTO PASTA SALAD

serves 4-6

Growing up, Elisa loved to help her maman in the garden, and every summer they had an abundance of zucchini, which meant coming up with creative new recipes like this pesto pasta. We like to serve this at room temperature, making it perfect to take with you. You can use a regular vegetable peeler to make the zucchini noodles—press lightly to get very thin strips. They're less common in the United States, but corn nuts were a popular ingredient when we lived in Spain, and they make a great alternative to traditional nuts. To make this into a more substantial meal, add chicken, and to make it gluten-free, substitute your favorite gluten-free pasta—we love it with corn-based versions.

Fine sea salt and freshly ground black pepper

1 pound (*450 g*) linguine

2 pounds (*900 g*) zucchini noodles (see Tip)

2 cups (*400 g*) Basil Pesto (recipe follows) or store-bought

1 avocado, peeled and smashed

1 cup (*75 g*) toasted salted corn nuts

1 cup (*100 g*) grated Parmesan cheese

1. Bring a medium pot of generously salted water to a boil. Add the linguine and cook according to the package directions, until al dente, about 8 minutes. Drain in a colander, shaking well to remove any excess water.

2. In a large bowl, combine the linguine and zucchini noodles. Add the pesto and toss to coat. Add the avocado and toss to coat the noodles and create a creamy sauce. Season to taste with salt and pepper.

3. Divide among four bowls, sprinkle with the corn nuts and Parmesan, and serve.

TIP: *To make your own zucchini noodles, trim 4 zucchini (about 2½ pounds / 1.1 kg), then use a mandoline, julienne peeler, or spiralizer to create the noodles.*

BASIL PESTO

MAKES ABOUT 2 CUPS (*400 g*)

6 cups (*180 g*) packed fresh basil leaves (see Tip)

2 garlic cloves, peeled

3 tablespoons fresh lemon juice (from 2 lemons)

¾ teaspoon fine sea salt

¾ teaspoon freshly ground black pepper

1 cup (*240 ml*) extra-virgin olive oil

¾ cup (*75 g*) grated Parmesan cheese

¾ cup (*75 g*) raw unsalted walnut halves

In a blender or food processor, combine the basil, garlic, lemon juice, salt, and pepper and blend, scraping down the bowl as needed, until the basil is finely chopped, about 1 minute. With the blender running on low, gradually add the olive oil and blend for about 1 minute to emulsify. Add the Parmesan and walnut halves and blend until mostly smooth, about 30 seconds more. Use right away or refrigerate in an airtight container, covered with a thin layer of olive oil, for up to 5 days or freeze for up to 1 month.

TIP: *If you want to make a more unusual pesto—or don't have enough basil—you can use other greens, such as arugula, mint, kale, or cilantro, in place of some or all of the basil.*

JULIA SALAD

CUMIN CHICKPEA SALAD
WITH ROASTED RED PEPPERS, FETA, AND SCALLIONS

serves 4-6

....

This Mediterranean-style salad was inspired by Ben's grandmother, who grew up in Algeria. Ben has vivid memories of her roasting peppers over an open flame until black and blistered and then peeling them by hand. We promise our method is far easier! Serve this zesty salad as a side dish or top it with tuna to make it a meal. It doesn't require additional dressing, but happens to be quite delicious with our balsamic vinaigrette (see page 125).

3 large red bell peppers (about 2 pounds / *900 g*), diced

¼ cup plus 2 tablespoons (*90 ml*) extra-virgin olive oil

1 teaspoon fine sea salt

3 (15.5-ounce / *439 g*) cans chickpeas, drained and rinsed

8 scallions, sliced

2 cups (*88 g*) packed mesclun or baby arugula

1½ cups (*230 g*) crumbled feta cheese

2 tablespoons ground cumin

½ teaspoon freshly ground black pepper

1. Preheat the oven to 400°F (*200°C*). Line a sheet pan with parchment paper.

2. In a large bowl, toss the red bell peppers with 2 tablespoons of the olive oil and ½ teaspoon of the salt. Spread in an even layer on the parchment-lined sheet pan and roast until the skins blister and the flesh is tender, 20 to 25 minutes. Let cool.

3. In a large bowl, combine the cooled peppers with the chickpeas, scallions, mesclun, and 1 cup (*150 g*) of the feta. Add the cumin, pepper, and the remaining ½ teaspoon salt and ¼ cup (*60 ml*) olive oil and toss to coat. Sprinkle with the remaining ½ cup (*80 g*) feta and serve.

notes

....
....
....
....
....
....

TAWNI SALAD

FARRO, SWEET POTATOES, RED CABBAGE, FETA, PICKLED ONIONS, AND FRIED EGGS

serves 4-6

....

This recipe is another original creation from our longtime head chef Tawni and features so many great flavors in one fantastic bowl—hearty farro, pungent pickled onions, and the comforting sweetness of roasted potatoes and cabbage. But the real star is the smoky-sweet hot sauce made with chipotle peppers in adobo and cocoa powder. It's a surprising twist on classic hot sauce and is so popular that we now sell it in jars at maman. To make this salad vegan, swap the feta and egg for avocado. You may have leftover pistou, which is excellent on toast or tossed with pasta for a quick meal.

KALE-PUMPKIN SEED PISTOU

2 cups (*80 g*) packed baby kale leaves

1 jalapeño (about 1½ ounces / *42 g*), seeded and roughly chopped

1 garlic clove, peeled

2 teaspoons fresh lemon juice

1 teaspoon ground cumin

1 teaspoon fine sea salt

1 cup (*240 ml*) extra-virgin olive oil

½ cup (*68 g*) toasted unsalted pumpkin seeds

SALAD

2 cups (*360 g*) Italian pearled farro

2 medium sweet potatoes (about 1½ pounds / *675 g*), cut into ½-inch (*1.25 cm*) chunks

5 tablespoons (*75 ml*) extra-virgin olive oil

Fine sea salt and freshly ground black pepper

¼ head red cabbage (about 12 ounces / *340 g*), cut into 1-inch (*2.5 cm*) chunks

1. Preheat the oven to 400°F (*200°C*). Line two sheet pans with parchment paper.

2. **MAKE THE KALE-PUMPKIN SEED PISTOU:** In a blender, combine the kale, jalapeño, garlic, lemon juice, cumin, salt, and ½ cup (*120 ml*) water and blend on medium-high for about 30 seconds to liquefy. With the motor running on medium-high, gradually add the olive oil. Add the pumpkin seeds, then slowly turn to high and blend until mostly smooth, about 1 minute.

3. **MAKE THE SALAD:** In a medium saucepan, combine the farro and 3 cups (*720 ml*) water, cover, and bring to a boil. Reduce the heat to medium and simmer, partially covered, until the grains are al dente and have absorbed most of the water, 17 to 20 minutes. Remove from the heat and fluff with a fork. Cover and let stand for at least 5 minutes.

4. Meanwhile, in a medium bowl, toss the sweet potato chunks with 2 tablespoons of the olive oil and ½ teaspoon salt. Spread in an even layer on one of the prepared sheet pans and roast until browned and softened, 20 to 25 minutes.

5. In the same bowl, toss the cabbage with 1 tablespoon of the olive oil and ½ teaspoon salt. Spread in an even layer on the other prepared sheet pan and roast until slightly crispy, about 20 minutes.

6. In a large bowl, combine the sweet potatoes, cabbage, farro, and 1 cup (*215 g*) of the kale-pumpkin seed pistou. Toss to coat, adding more pistou as needed.

RECIPE AND INGREDIENTS CONTINUE

4 to 6 large eggs

¾ cup (*105 g*) sheep's milk feta cheese (such as Meredith Dairy)

2 cups (*200 g*) pickled red onions (see Pickled Vegetables, page 104)

4 ounces (*113 g*) packed microgreens or fresh herbs (optional)

Smoky Cocoa Hot Sauce (recipe follows)

7. Heat the remaining 2 tablespoons olive oil in a large nonstick skillet over medium heat. When the oil is shimmering, crack the eggs into the pan, season with some salt and pepper, and fry until the whites are set but the yolks are still runny, about 3 minutes.

8. Divide the farro and vegetable mixture among four to six bowls and sprinkle with the feta. Top each bowl with pickled onions and 1 fried egg. Garnish with microgreens or fresh herbs (if using) and serve with the hot sauce alongside.

SMOKY COCOA HOT SAUCE

MAKES 3 CUPS (*720 ml*)

¼ cup (*70 g*) canned chipotle peppers in adobo sauce

½ red onion (about 5½ ounces / *154 g*), chopped

2 garlic cloves, peeled

1 cup (*240 ml*) cold water

⅔ cup (*150 ml*) white wine vinegar

3 tablespoons unsweetened natural cocoa powder

1 tablespoon plus 1 teaspoon fine sea salt

2 teaspoons sugar

notes

In a blender, combine the chipotles, onion, garlic, cold water, vinegar, cocoa, salt, and sugar and blend on high until completely smooth, 1 to 2 minutes. Store refrigerated in an airtight container for up to 2 weeks.

when to use what: blender vs. immersion blender vs. food processor

Apart from the stand mixer—which is indispensable for all the baking we do!—the most useful appliances in our kitchen are those for breaking down and blending ingredients: the blender, immersion blender, and food processor. Sometimes they can be used interchangeably, but at other times, there really is only one tool for the job at hand. Our recipes always note when you can make a swap. Here's a quick guide to getting the most out of these kitchen workhorses.

BLENDER When a dish needs to be uniformly pureed or silky smooth, reach for a blender, which works best for liquids and blending soups and smoothies.

IMMERSION BLENDER Though not as powerful as a traditional blender, an immersion blender is easy to use and clean and is super compact, making it great for small kitchens. It works wonderfully for soups, sauces, or any dish with a lot of liquid, but isn't ideal for breaking up tough veggies or large pieces of food.

FOOD PROCESSOR With rigid, razor-sharp blades, a food processor is perfect for prepping veggies and making chunky sauces, but it doesn't work as well when there is a lot of liquid or when you're looking for a super smooth texture.

SWEET CORN SOUP

serves 4

....

When Elisa was growing up, corn was a family favorite, especially in the summer when her mom, Janice, stopped by the local farm. The Marshalls often enjoyed corn on the cob, but Janice also channeled her creative side to make dishes like this soup. Despite including just a few simple ingredients—things you probably have on hand—it is bursting with flavor and is a guaranteed crowd-pleaser. Corn nuts are a bit unexpected, but they add great crunchy texture—acting almost like croutons—and are a fun way to highlight this soup's main ingredient. Use vegetable broth to make it vegan or add a swirl of heavy cream or a dollop of goat cheese to take it in a more luxurious direction. Fresh corn is always going to taste best, but this soup can be made year-round with canned or frozen.

1¾ pounds (*785 g*) fresh or frozen corn kernels (from 6 to 8 ears) or 4½ cups (*785 g*) drained canned corn, plus more for garnish

1 onion (about 11 ounces / *310 g*), diced

1 garlic clove, chopped

2 large fresh rosemary sprigs

3 cups (*720 ml*) vegetable or chicken broth

Fine sea salt and freshly ground black pepper

¼ cup (*60 ml*) extra-virgin olive oil

Toasted salted corn nuts, fresh lime juice, and fresh basil, cilantro, or parsley, for garnish

1. In a large pot, combine the corn, onion, garlic, rosemary, and broth and season with salt and pepper. Bring to a boil over high heat and boil, stirring occasionally, for 10 minutes. Reduce the heat to medium-low, cover, and cook for 30 to 40 minutes to allow the flavors to meld. Remove the pot from the heat, let the soup cool for about 15 minutes, and discard the rosemary.

2. Transfer the soup to a blender. With the blender running on medium-high, gradually add the olive oil and blend for about 30 seconds to fully incorporate the oil. (Depending on the size of your blender, you may need to do this in batches. Alternatively, use an immersion blender to blend in the pot.) Leave the soup a bit chunky or continue blending to give it a smoother consistency if you prefer.

3. Return the soup to the pot and warm over medium heat for 5 to 7 minutes. Season to taste with salt and pepper.

4. Ladle the soup into bowls, garnish with more corn kernels, along with corn nuts, lime juice, and fresh herbs, and serve.

notes

....
....
....
....
....

ROASTED CARROT SOUP

serves 6-8

Sweet potato highlights the sweetness of carrots and helps make this vivid orange soup extra thick and creamy. In fact, the sweet potato does such a good job that you can swap out heavy cream for lighter options like coconut milk, whole milk, or even almond milk if you like. We love the soup as is, especially with a crisp winter salad on the side, but it's also a great canvas for your culinary imagination. If you're using coconut milk, try adding fresh lime juice and cilantro to give it an Asian-inspired twist. Alternatively, bump up the ginger and add some curry powder for a more deeply spiced version. If you're lucky enough to find heirloom carrots, keep in mind that they are usually thinner and may roast more quickly.

3 pounds (*1.3 kg*) carrots (about 20 carrots), cut into rounds ½ inch (*1.25 cm*) thick

5 tablespoons (*75 ml*) extra-virgin olive oil

1 bunch fresh thyme (about *15 g*), leaves picked

1 bunch fresh rosemary (about *15 g*), needles picked

Fine sea salt and freshly ground black pepper

1 large sweet potato (about 1 pound / *450 g*), peeled and cut into ½-inch (*1.25 cm*) cubes

1 onion (about 11 ounces / *310 g*), very thinly sliced

1 garlic clove, chopped

2 teaspoons grated fresh ginger

2 tablespoons dry red wine

2 cups (*480 ml*) vegetable or chicken broth

4 cups (*960 ml*) heavy cream

Crème fraîche and fresh flat-leaf parsley leaves, for garnish

notes

1. Preheat the oven to 400°F (*200°C*). Line two sheet pans with parchment paper.

2. In a large bowl, combine the carrots, 3 tablespoons of the olive oil, and about three-quarters each of the thyme leaves and rosemary needles. Season with salt and pepper and toss to combine. Spread in an even layer on one of the prepared sheet pans and roast until browned and softened, 30 to 45 minutes. Let cool for about 15 minutes.

3. Meanwhile, in a small bowl, combine the sweet potato, 1 tablespoon of the olive oil, and the remaining thyme and rosemary. Season with salt and pepper and toss to combine. Spread in an even layer on the other prepared sheet pan and roast until browned and softened, 25 to 30 minutes. Let cool for about 15 minutes.

4. While the vegetables are roasting, heat the remaining 1 tablespoon olive oil in a small nonstick skillet over medium heat. When the oil is shimmering, add the onion and cook, stirring frequently, until soft and translucent, about 10 minutes. If the onion sticks to the bottom of the pan, add a few tablespoons of water to deglaze the pan. Add the garlic and ginger and cook, stirring frequently, for about 1 minute. Reduce the heat to medium-low and add the red wine to deglaze the pan, using a wooden spoon to scrape up any browned bits from the bottom. Continue to cook, stirring frequently, until the wine has been absorbed and the onion is golden brown, about 10 minutes. Remove the pan from the heat and let cool for about 10 minutes.

5. Transfer the cooled carrots, sweet potatoes, and onions to a blender, and with the blender running

on medium, gradually add the broth and blend until completely smooth, about 1 minute. (Alternatively, transfer the vegetables to a large pot and use an immersion blender to blend in the broth.)

6. Transfer the soup to a large pot (if it's not there already), add the heavy cream, and warm over medium heat, stirring occasionally, for 5 to 7 minutes to heat through. Season to taste with salt and pepper.

7. Ladle the soup into bowls, garnish with crème fraîche and parsley, and serve.

TIP: *To store fresh ginger, peel it with a vegetable peeler, seal it tightly in a freezer-safe bag, and freeze. When ready to use, remove the ginger from the freezer and use a fine grater to grate as much as you need.*

GREEN HERB VELOUTÉ

serves 2-4

....

Velouté is French for "velvety," which perfectly describes this comforting soup, inspired by one Elisa's maman makes. Packed with leafy greens and fragrant herbs, it is bright and flavorful, and wildly good for you. It's also vegan and gluten-free and incredibly easy to make. We love this soup chilled or at room temperature—and if you don't need it to be vegan, topped with a dollop of cheese as well as sprinkled with lemon zest and fresh chives. Serve smaller portions in beautiful vintage glasses to show off the vivid green hue and garnish with florals for special occasions.

1 tablespoon extra-virgin olive oil, plus more for drizzling

8 scallions, thinly sliced

Fine sea salt and freshly ground black pepper

4 cups (*about 150 g*) packed mixed greens, such as spinach, arugula, dandelion, and/or watercress, stems removed

4 cups (*960 ml*) vegetable broth

¼ cup (*18 g*) packed sliced fresh chives, plus more for garnish

¼ cup (*6 g*) packed fresh flat-leaf parsley leaves

2 tablespoons fresh chervil or tarragon leaves

1 tablespoon fresh mint leaves

3 ounces (*84 g*) Brousse or other soft cheese, for garnish (optional)

1. Fill a large bowl with ice.

2. Heat the olive oil in a large saucepan over medium heat. When the oil is shimmering, add the scallions, season with salt, and cook until soft, 1 to 2 minutes. Add the greens and broth, season with salt and pepper, and bring to a boil. Cook until the greens are slightly wilted and soft, about 3 minutes, then add the chives, parsley, chervil, and mint and cook for about 1 minute more to just wilt the herbs.

3. Transfer the soup to a blender and blend until very smooth, about 1 minute. (Alternatively, use an immersion blender directly in the pan.) Transfer to a medium metal bowl, set the metal bowl inside the large bowl of ice, and let stand, stirring occasionally, to cool the soup and set its bright green color.

4. Divide the soup between two bowls or four smaller glasses. Top with the Brousse (if using), garnish with chives, and drizzle with olive oil. Serve.

TIP: *Velouté can also be refrigerated until cold and served chilled.*

notes

SUMMER STRAWBERRY GAZPACHO

serves 4

This strawberry-infused gazpacho is a variation on the one we ate almost daily while living in Ibiza. It makes the most refreshing lunch on hot days and is also lovely served in small glasses as a predinner treat. Strawberries are not traditional in this dish, but their sweetness means you can make this soup even if you don't have perfectly ripe tomatoes.

5 cups (*800 g*) chopped vine-ripened tomatoes (about 7 tomatoes)

2 cups (*330 g*) hulled and quartered strawberries, plus more for garnish

1 English cucumber (about 12½ ounces / *350 g*), peeled and chopped

2 garlic cloves, peeled

1 jalapeño (*about 30 g*), seeded and chopped

1 cup (*30 g*) packed fresh basil leaves, chopped, plus more for garnish

½ cup (*120 ml*) extra-virgin olive oil

2 tablespoons apple cider vinegar

Fine sea salt and freshly ground black pepper

1 cup (*160 g*) soft and crumbly goat's milk cheese

1 tablespoon plus 1 teaspoon grated lime zest

1. In a blender, combine the tomatoes, strawberries, cucumber, garlic, jalapeño, basil, olive oil, vinegar, 1 teaspoon salt, and 1 teaspoon pepper and blend until smooth, about 1 minute. Transfer to an airtight container and refrigerate for at least 1 hour and up to 4 days.

2. In a small bowl, toss together the goat cheese and lime zest to create a crumbly mixture. Season to taste with salt and pepper.

3. Ladle the chilled soup into four bowls, season to taste with salt and pepper, and sprinkle each with the goat cheese mixture and strawberries or fresh basil. Serve immediately.

notes

RED WINE, MUSHROOM, AND ONION SOUP

serves 6

French onion soup is a classic and very common in Montreal, where we met. Our version includes mushrooms, which make for a heartier bowl. It's vegan, but we've been known to add Comté or Gruyère and gratinée the top, and at maman, we serve it with a grilled cheese sandwich for dipping. The wine is an important player here: We love to use a dry red from the Languedoc region, where Ben grew up.

2 tablespoons extra-virgin olive oil

2 red onions (about 1⅓ pounds / 620 g), very thinly sliced

2 garlic cloves, chopped

1¾ cups (420 ml) dry red wine

¼ cup (36 g) all-purpose flour

8 cups (1.9 liters) vegetable broth

1½ pounds (675 g) cremini mushrooms, trimmed and sliced

25 fresh thyme sprigs, tied together in a bouquet, plus fresh thyme leaves for garnish

1 tablespoon dried thyme

1 tablespoon fine sea salt

¼ teaspoon freshly ground black pepper

1. Heat the olive oil in a large pot over medium heat. When the oil is shimmering, add the red onions, reduce the heat to low, and cook, stirring frequently and covering when not stirring, until pale pink and translucent, about 10 minutes. Add the garlic and cook, stirring frequently and covering when not stirring, until the onions are browned and sticking to the pot, about 35 minutes.

2. Add 1 cup (240 ml) of the wine to deglaze the pot, using a wooden spoon to scrape any browned bits from the bottom. Increase the heat to medium and cook, stirring frequently, until the wine has been absorbed and the pot is almost dry. Add the flour and cook, stirring frequently, until the flour has turned light brown, about 1 minute.

3. Add the broth, whisking to get all the flour and onions off the bottom of the pot. Add the mushrooms and fresh thyme bouquet, increase the heat to high, and bring to a boil. Reduce the heat to medium-low and add the dried thyme, salt, pepper, and the remaining ¾ cup (180 ml) red wine. Simmer for at least 30 minutes to deepen the flavor.

4. Discard the thyme bouquet. Ladle the soup into bowls, garnish with fresh thyme leaves, and serve.

notes

POTATO, LEEK, AND SUNCHOKE SOUP
WITH ROSEMARY OIL

serves 6-8

....

To make classic potato-leek soup a bit more interesting, we add sunchokes, also known as Jerusalem artichokes, which are the root end of a plant in the sunflower family. These bumpy brown-skinned tubers add sweetness and mild nuttiness, while homemade rosemary oil lends woody, herbal notes. You'll have plenty of rosemary oil left over, and its uses are almost endless—drizzle it on everything from pizza and pasta to hummus and burrata, or use it in place of butter on toast. We leave the skins on both the potatoes and the sunchokes, which adds specks of color to the soup, makes it more nutritious, and is a whole lot easier, but you can peel them if you prefer a more velvety soup. To make this soup vegan, use a nondairy milk.

ROSEMARY OIL

2 cups (*480 ml*) extra-virgin olive oil

¾ cup (*24 g*) packed fresh rosemary needles

¼ teaspoon fine sea salt

SOUP

1 tablespoon extra-virgin olive oil

1 yellow onion (about 11 ounces / *310 g*), diced

2 large leeks (about 1¼ pounds / *560 g*), dark green tops reserved, white and light green parts sliced into rings and well washed (see Tip, page 67)

2 garlic cloves, chopped

1½ pounds (*675 g*) sunchokes, roughly chopped

1½ pounds (*675 g*) Yukon Gold potatoes, diced

8 cups (*1.9 liters*) vegetable broth

1 tablespoon fresh lemon juice

1 large fresh rosemary sprig

2 teaspoons dried thyme

Fine sea salt and freshly ground black pepper

½ cup (*120 ml*) whole milk

1. **MAKE THE ROSEMARY OIL:** In a blender, combine the olive oil, rosemary, and salt and blend on high until the rosemary is very finely chopped, about 30 seconds. Pour through a fine-mesh sieve or cheesecloth set over an airtight container; discard the rosemary. (The rosemary oil can be refrigerated in an airtight container for up to 1 month.)

2. **MAKE THE SOUP:** Heat the olive oil in a large pot over medium heat. When the oil is shimmering, add the onion and sliced leeks and cook, stirring occasionally, until starting to turn translucent, about 5 minutes. Add the garlic and cook, stirring occasionally, until the onions and leeks are softened and completely translucent, about 15 minutes.

3. Add the sunchokes, potatoes, and broth and stir to get the onions off the bottom of the pot. Add the lemon juice, rosemary, thyme, dark green leek tops, 2 tablespoons salt, and ½ teaspoon pepper and bring to a boil. Reduce the heat to medium and simmer until the potatoes and sunchokes are easily pierced with a fork, about 15 minutes. Let cool slightly, then discard the rosemary sprig and leek tops.

4. Set aside about 2 cups (*480 ml*) of the soup. Working in batches, transfer the rest of the soup to a blender and blend until very smooth. Return the pureed soup, along with the reserved soup, to the pot. (Alternatively, use an immersion blender directly in the pot, then return the reserved 2 cups.) Whisk in the milk, season to taste with salt, and bring to a simmer over medium-low heat.

5. Ladle the soup into bowls, drizzle with the rosemary oil, and serve.

white chocolate, blueberry
and lavender naked cake
(page 181)

PART III

Sweets

vanilla oatmeal raisin
cookies (page 157)

and Sips

cookies and bars

"What I hope to pass along to my kids about cooking, baking, and food: It is not actually about the cooking, or the baking, or even the food, because making a meal can be one of the most meaningful ways to explore the depths of your own creativity, doing it for someone else can be one of the most acute ways to express how much you care for them, and sharing it can foster such a meaningful connectedness that its nourishment overrides the actual making, doing, or eating. Unless, that is, there is a plate of nutty chocolate chip cookies on the table. Pun intended."

—Leandra Medine Cohen,
writer and cookie consumer

TIPS:

For the most consistent results, we set a rack in the center of the oven and bake one sheet pan of cookies at a time, but you can set racks in the upper and lower positions and bake two sheet pans of cookies simultaneously. Or, if your oven allows, you can set two sheet pans side by side on the center rack. Everyone's oven is unique, so be sure to rotate your sheet pans—either from front to back or from one rack to another for even baking.

Store the baked cookies at room temperature in an airtight container for up to 2 days. You can refrigerate the balls of dough for up to 7 days or freeze them for up to 3 months in a double layer of resealable plastic bags. The cookies can be baked straight from the freezer but may require an extra minute in the oven.

MAMAN'S NUTTY CHOCOLATE CHIP COOKIES

makes 14 cookies

....

This is the cookie that put maman on the culinary map! We've shipped thousands across the country for weddings, birthdays, anniversaries, and—our favorite—"just because I love you" gifts. Gooey on the inside, crisp on the outside, salty, crunchy, and sweet, these cookies even earned a spot on Oprah's Favorite Things list in 2017. The dough keeps in the refrigerator for 7 days or in the freezer for 3 months (see Tip), so you can bake cookies whenever a craving strikes.

11 ounces (*310 g*) dark chocolate baking wafers (such as Guittard)

2 sticks (8 ounces / *225 g*) unsalted butter, at room temperature

1 cup (*135 g*) raw unsalted macadamia nuts

½ cup (*56 g*) sliced raw unsalted almonds

½ cup (*50 g*) raw unsalted walnut halves

1¾ cups (*298 g*) packed light brown sugar

2¼ cups (*326 g*) all-purpose flour

2 teaspoons fine sea salt

2 large eggs

notes

....
....
....
....
....
....
....

1. In a stand mixer fitted with the paddle attachment, combine the baking wafers, butter, macadamia nuts, almonds, and walnut halves and mix on low for about 30 seconds to break down the nuts and chocolate a bit. Add the brown sugar and mix on low until the butter and sugar come together. With the mixer still running on low, gradually add the flour and salt and mix until incorporated. Add the eggs, 1 at a time, scraping down the sides of the bowl after each addition, and mix until the dough starts sticking to the sides of the bowl. Scrape down the sides of the bowl again and mix on low for 10 seconds more to evenly distribute the nuts and chocolate.

2. Turn the dough out onto a large sheet of parchment paper and flatten into a square roughly 1 inch (*2.5 cm*) thick. Fold the parchment paper to completely cover and wrap the dough, place in a resealable plastic bag, and refrigerate for at least 1 hour and up to 7 days.

3. Set a rack in the center of the oven and preheat to 350°F (*180°C*). Line a sheet pan with parchment paper.

4. Divide the chilled dough into 14 equal portions (about 3½ ounces/*100 g* each) and using your hands, roll each portion into a ball. Arrange 7 balls of dough on the prepared sheet pan, spacing them about 3 inches (*7.5 cm*) apart, then use the palm of your hand to flatten into disks roughly ½ inch (*1.25 cm*) thick. Bake for 6 minutes. Rotate the sheet pan as needed for even baking (see Tip) and bake until the edges are browned but the centers are still a little gooey, 6 to 7 minutes longer. Let cool on the sheet pan for 10 minutes, then enjoy right away or transfer to a wire rack and let cool completely. Repeat with the remaining cookie dough.

CHOCOLATE SANDWICH COOKIES
WITH FLEUR DE SEL AND WHITE CHOCOLATE CRÈME

makes 20-24 sandwich cookies

We all know and love Oreo cookies, but—blame it on our French influence—we thought we could do just a little bit better. Our version is reminiscent of the classic after-school snack but doubles down on the buttery, chocolaty notes and is finished with fleur de sel.

CHOCOLATE COOKIES

¾ cup (*109 g*) all-purpose flour

¼ cup (*20 g*) unsweetened natural cocoa powder

1 teaspoon fleur de sel

1 stick (4 ounces / *113 g*) unsalted butter, at room temperature

½ cup (*90 g*) packed light brown sugar

3 tablespoons granulated sugar

WHITE CHOCOLATE CRÈME

1½ ounces (*42 g*) white chocolate, chopped, or ⅓ cup (*42 g*) white chocolate chips

1½ sticks (6 ounces / *170 g*) unsalted butter, at room temperature

⅔ cup (*87 g*) confectioners' sugar

1 teaspoon pure vanilla extract

notes

1. **MAKE THE CHOCOLATE COOKIES:** In a small bowl, whisk together the flour, cocoa powder, and fleur de sel.

2. In a stand mixer fitted with the paddle attachment, combine the butter, brown sugar, and granulated sugar and beat on medium-low, scraping down the sides of the bowl as needed, until fully combined, about 5 minutes. Add the flour mixture and mix on low until a crumbly dough forms.

3. Turn out the dough onto a clean work surface. Press into a disk ½ inch (*1.25 cm*) thick, wrap tightly in plastic wrap, and refrigerate for at least 1 hour and up to 48 hours. (If the dough is refrigerated for longer than 1 hour, let it stand at room temperature for about 15 minutes before rolling.)

4. Set a rack in the center of the oven; preheat to 350°F (*180°C*). Line two sheet pans with parchment paper.

5. On a lightly floured work surface, use a rolling pin to roll out the dough to about a ⅛-inch (*3 mm*) thickness. If the dough cracks, use your fingers to pinch it back together. Using a 1¾-inch (*4.25 cm*) round cookie cutter, cut the dough into rounds. Gather up the scraps of dough, form into a disk, and refrigerate for at least 30 minutes before rolling again and cutting out more rounds.

6. Arrange the cookies on the prepared sheet pans, spacing them about 1 inch (*2.5 cm*) apart, and freeze for 10 minutes.

7. Transfer one sheet pan to the oven and bake, rotating the sheet pan as needed for even baking (see Tip, page 150), until crisp around the edges with a slight give in the center, 8 to 10 minutes. Let cool on the sheet pan for 2 minutes, then transfer to a wire rack to cool completely, about 20 minutes. Repeat to bake the remaining cookies.

8. **MEANWHILE, MAKE THE WHITE CHOCOLATE CRÈME:** In a double boiler, or in a heatproof medium bowl set over a pan of simmering water, melt the white

chocolate, stirring as needed. (Alternatively, place the white chocolate in a microwave-safe bowl and microwave in 30-second intervals, stirring after each interval, until fully melted.) Set aside to cool slightly.

TIP: *The cookies can be stored in an airtight container and refrigerated for up to 5 days. Bring to room temperature before serving.*

9. In a stand mixer fitted with the paddle attachment, combine the butter and confectioners' sugar and beat on low until fully combined, about 1 minute. Increase the speed to medium and beat until very smooth, about 3 minutes. With the mixer still running on medium, gradually add the melted white chocolate, followed by the vanilla, and beat for 2 minutes to thoroughly combine.

10. Transfer the crème to a piping bag fitted with a medium round tip. (Alternatively, spoon the crème into a resealable plastic bag and snip off a bottom corner so there is a small opening.) Pipe about 1 tablespoon of crème onto the flat side of half of the cooled cookies. Top each with another cookie to make sandwiches.

GRANDMA GRACIE'S SHORTBREAD COOKIES

makes 24 cookies

....

Elisa likes to say that in her grandmother Gracie's kitchen, everything is made with love and an extra spoonful of sugar. Gracie, Elisa's maman's maman, has five children and eleven grandchildren and always manages to surprise them with baked goods, hidden under a silver cloche on her dining room table. As kids, Elisa and her sister always hoped to find these buttery shortbread cookies, which they called snowball cookies. The recipe is simple and very flexible. Elisa's maman makes hers with semisweet chocolate, but you can play with different kinds of chocolate, nuts, candy, or citrus zest. You can also roll out the dough and cut it into shapes. Every time Elisa bakes a batch, it brings her right back to Gracie's kitchen.

3 cups (*435 g*) all-purpose flour

½ cup (*60 g*) cornstarch

4 sticks (1 pound / *450 g*) unsalted butter, at room temperature (see Tip)

½ teaspoon almond extract

1½ cups (*195 g*) confectioners' sugar

5 ounces (*140 g*) semisweet chocolate, chopped, or ¾ cup (*140 g*) semisweet chocolate chips

TIPS:
Did you forget to soften the butter? Elisa's maman taught her a great trick: Grate a hard stick of butter on the coarse side of a box grater to instantly soften the butter, making it the perfect temperature for baking.

Store the cookies at room temperature in an airtight container for up to 1 week.

notes

1. Set a rack in the center of the oven and preheat to 300°F (*150°C*). Line two sheet pans with parchment paper.

2. In a medium bowl, sift together the flour and cornstarch.

3. In a stand mixer fitted with the paddle attachment, beat the butter on medium until creamy, about 3 minutes. Add the almond extract. With the mixer running on low, gradually add 1 cup (*130 g*) of the confectioners' sugar and continue beating for about 1 minute to fully combine. Increase the speed to high and beat until light and fluffy, about 3 minutes more. Add the flour mixture in 3 batches and beat on medium for about 2 minutes to fully combine. Fold in the chocolate.

4. Using your hands, roll the dough into 1½- to 2-inch (*3.75 to 5 cm*) balls and arrange on the prepared sheet pans about 2 inches (*5 cm*) apart. Transfer one sheet pan to the oven and bake, rotating the sheet pan as needed for even baking (see Tip, page 150), until the bottoms are light brown—the tops will remain pale—20 to 25 minutes. Transfer the cookies to a wire rack and let cool completely, about 30 minutes. Repeat to bake the remaining cookies.

5. Meanwhile, place the remaining ½ cup (*65 g*) confectioners' sugar in a wide, shallow bowl. Set a wire rack inside a sheet pan.

6. Roll the cooled cookies in the confectioners' sugar, then place on the rack.

VANILLA OATMEAL RAISIN COOKIES

makes 24 cookies

....

The genius of these cookies, which come from our former pastry chef Vanessa Sakosky, is that they are almost infinitely adaptable. We've substituted dried cherries for the raisins and we seriously doubt anyone would complain if you tossed a handful of chocolate chips into the dough. You can also play around with different spices to give these cookies more seasonal or holiday appeal. In fall, we add ¾ teaspoon pumpkin pie spice, while for Christmas, we add ¾ teaspoon ground ginger, plus sprinkle some finely chopped candied ginger on top. Whichever version you bake, these cookies have the most incredible aroma. We like the scent so much, we turned it into a candle so we could enjoy it without ever even turning on the oven!

1½ cups (*140 g*) old-fashioned oats

1 cup (*145 g*) all-purpose flour

½ cup (*73 g*) raisins

½ teaspoon ground cinnamon

½ teaspoon baking soda

½ teaspoon fine sea salt

1 stick (4 ounces / *113 g*) unsalted butter, at room temperature

½ cup (*100 g*) granulated sugar

½ cup (*90 g*) packed light brown sugar

¾ teaspoon pure vanilla extract

1 large egg

1. In a medium bowl, whisk together the oats, flour, raisins, cinnamon, baking soda, and salt.

2. In a stand mixer fitted with the paddle attachment, combine the butter, granulated sugar, brown sugar, and vanilla and beat on medium, scraping down the sides of the bowl as needed, until fully combined, about 3 minutes. With the mixer running on low, add the egg and beat until fully incorporated, about 2 minutes. Add the flour mixture and mix on low just until no flour is visible, about 1 minute. Cover the bowl tightly with plastic wrap and refrigerate the dough for at least 1 hour and up to 2 days. (If the dough is refrigerated for longer than 1 hour, let it stand for 15 minutes before scooping.)

3. Set a rack in the center of the oven and preheat to 350°F (*180°C*). Line two sheet pans with parchment paper.

4. Scoop heaping tablespoons of dough onto the parchment-lined sheet pans, spacing them 2 inches (*5 cm*) apart. Transfer one sheet pan to the oven and bake, rotating the sheet pan as needed for even baking (see Tip, page 150), until the tops start to turn golden but the centers are still a little gooey, 10 to 12 minutes. Let the cookies cool on the sheet pan for 2 minutes, then transfer to a wire rack to cool. Repeat to bake the remaining cookies.

TIP: *Store the cookies at room temperature in an airtight container for up to 5 days.*

notes

CHOCOLATE-HAZELNUT BROWNIES

makes 12-16 brownies

....

These brownies reach the next level thanks to everyone's favorite spread, Nutella!
Addictively chocolaty, chewy, and dense, these brownies are a year-round staple at maman
and are often requested for events—we cut them into mini squares to make the perfect bite.
Though they're incredibly rich and delicious as is, sometimes we top these dark beauties
with confectioners' sugar, salted caramel, or even more Nutella.

Vegetable oil spray

1½ cups (*218 g*) all-purpose flour

½ teaspoon baking powder

¼ teaspoon fine sea salt

2 cups (*580 g*) chocolate-hazelnut
spread (such as Nutella; see Tip)

¾ cup (*150 g*) sugar

2½ sticks (10 ounces / *280 g*)
unsalted butter, melted and
cooled slightly

4 large eggs

1. Set a rack in the center of the oven and preheat to
350°F (*180°C*). Coat a 9 × 13-inch (*23 × 33 cm*) baking
pan with vegetable oil spray.

2. In a medium bowl, whisk together the flour,
baking powder, and salt.

3. In a stand mixer fitted with the paddle attachment,
combine the chocolate-hazelnut spread, sugar, and
melted butter and mix on low for about 3 minutes to
fully combine. With the mixer running on low, add
the eggs, 1 at a time, scraping down the sides of the
bowl after each addition and beating until the eggs
are fully incorporated, about 4 minutes total. Add
the flour mixture and mix on low, scraping down
the sides of the bowl as needed, just until no flour is
visible, about 1 minute.

4. Transfer the batter to the prepared pan and
smooth out the top. Bake until a toothpick inserted
in the center comes out clean, 25 to 30 minutes. Let
cool in the pan on a wire rack for 30 minutes before
cutting into 12 to 16 brownies.

TIPS:
*When measuring sticky ingredients like Nutella,
nut butters, or caramel, try coating your spoon,
spatula, and measuring cup with a thin layer of
vegetable oil spray for easier cleanup.*

*Store the brownies refrigerated in an airtight
container for up to 5 days.*

notes

TIPS:

When pressing dough into a pan, as here, or rolling it into balls, coat your hands with a little bit of vegetable oil spray or dust them with flour to prevent sticking.

Store the bars at room temperature in an airtight container for up to 4 days.

S'MORES COOKIE BARS

makes 12-16 bars

....

A hybrid of two beloved sweets—cookies and s'mores—these bars are a twist on maman's highly sought-after s'mores cookies. Studded with gooey, chewy marshmallows, crisp graham crackers, and a double hit of chocolate, this recipe delivers all the taste and texture of the campfire classic without the fuss or mess of toasting marshmallows over a flame. We love that these can be whipped up quickly and easily and that you can cut off a tiny bite whenever a craving hits or go for a larger square when you want to indulge.

1½ cups (*218 g*) all-purpose flour

½ teaspoon fine sea salt

¼ teaspoon baking powder

6 whole graham crackers, chopped into roughly ½-inch (*1.25 cm*) pieces

2 sticks (8 ounces / *225 g*) unsalted butter, at room temperature

¾ cup (*150 g*) granulated sugar

¾ cup (*128 g*) packed light brown sugar

¾ teaspoon pure vanilla extract

2 large eggs

1 cup (*155 g*) dark chocolate baking wafers (such as Guittard)

1 cup (*60 g*) mini marshmallows

2 ounces (*57 g*) dark chocolate, roughly chopped

notes

1. Set a rack in the center of the oven and preheat to 350°F (*180°C*). Line a 9 × 13-inch (*23 × 33 cm*) baking pan with parchment paper, leaving about 1 inch (*2.5 cm*) hanging over the long sides.

2. In a medium bowl, whisk together the flour, salt, and baking powder. Add the graham cracker pieces and stir to incorporate.

3. In a stand mixer fitted with the paddle attachment, combine the butter, granulated sugar, brown sugar, and vanilla and beat on medium, scraping down the sides of the bowl as needed, for about 3 minutes to fully combine. With the mixer running on low, add the eggs, 1 at a time, scraping down the sides of the bowl after each addition and beating until fully incorporated, about 2 minutes total. Add the flour mixture and mix on low just until no flour is visible, about 1 minute. Add the baking wafers and ½ cup (*30 g*) of the mini marshmallows and fold with a wooden spoon for about 30 seconds to evenly distribute.

4. Transfer the mixture to the prepared pan and using your hands, press it in evenly (see Tip). Bake until the sides start to brown but the center is still soft, 20 to 25 minutes. Sprinkle the chopped dark chocolate and the remaining ½ cup (*30 g*) marshmallows on top and continue baking until the marshmallows start to brown, 8 to 10 minutes more.

5. Transfer to a rack and let cool for 5 minutes in the pan, then pull on the parchment paper to remove from the pan. Place on the rack and let cool completely, about 1 hour. Cut into 12 to 16 bars and enjoy.

PUMPKIN-MAPLE MADELEINES

makes 18 madeleines

....

Flavoring classic French madeleines with pumpkin, an American favorite, and maple syrup, an iconic Canadian ingredient, is a perfect fusion of our cultures. One of the secrets to mastering madeleines is to let the dough chill overnight, so be patient! We use pumpkin pie spice, but you can swap equal parts cinnamon, nutmeg, ginger, and cloves. Madeleines have a beautiful shape, reminiscent of seashells; dipped in white chocolate and sprinkled with chopped pecans, they are even more tempting. You'll need to invest in madeleine pans to make this recipe, but after you make these delicate treats just once, you'll be happy you did.

1 cup (*145 g*) all-purpose flour

2 teaspoons pumpkin pie spice

1 teaspoon baking powder

½ teaspoon fine sea salt

½ cup (*120 ml*) whole milk

⅓ cup (*75 g*) canned pure pumpkin puree

¼ cup (*60 ml*) maple syrup

2 large eggs

¼ cup (*50 g*) sugar

1 stick (4 ounces / *113 g*) unsalted butter, melted (see Tip)

Vegetable oil spray

4½ ounces (*126 g*) white chocolate, chopped, or 1 cup (*126 g*) white chocolate chips

¼ cup (*30 g*) raw unsalted pecans, finely chopped

notes

1. In a small bowl, whisk together the flour, pumpkin pie spice, baking powder, and salt.

2. In a small saucepan, bring the milk, pumpkin puree, and maple syrup to a boil over high heat, keeping a close eye.

3. Meanwhile, in a stand mixer fitted with the whisk attachment, whip the eggs and sugar until fully combined and pale yellow, about 3 minutes. With the mixer running on low, gradually add the hot milk mixture and continue to whip for about 2 minutes to fully combine. Add the flour mixture in 4 batches, whipping until fully incorporated after each batch, about 3 minutes total. Add the melted butter and whip on low until the butter is fully incorporated and the dough is smooth, about 3 minutes. Cover and refrigerate for at least 24 hours and up to 48 hours.

4. Set a rack in the center of the oven and preheat to 425°F (*218°C*). Coat two standard madeleine pans with vegetable oil spray. Use a pastry brush to make sure all the crevices are well coated.

5. Stir the dough, then fill each madeleine mold about three-quarters of the way. Bake for 5 minutes, then reduce the oven temperature to 350°F (*180°C*) and continue baking until the tops are dark golden brown and a toothpick inserted in the center of the madeleines comes out clean, about 10 minutes more. Invert the pans and gently tap them to remove the madeleines. Set them on a wire rack to cool for about 30 minutes.

6. Set a wire rack inside a sheet pan.

7. In a double boiler, or in a heatproof bowl set over a pan of simmering water, melt the white chocolate, stirring as needed. (Alternatively, place the white

TIPS:

*If you don't have unsalted butter
on hand, you can use salted as long
as you eliminate or scale back how
much salt you use. Most baking
recipes require ½ teaspoon salt for
every 1 stick (4 ounces / 113 g) of
unsalted butter.*

*Store madeleines at room
temperature in an airtight container
for up to 3 days or individually
wrapped in plastic wrap and frozen
for up to 1 month.*

chocolate in a microwave-safe bowl and microwave
in 30-second intervals, stirring after each interval,
until fully melted.)

8. Holding the madeleines at an angle, dip the
top two-thirds of each one into the melted white
chocolate and place on the rack. While the chocolate
is still warm, sprinkle the chopped pecans on top.
Refrigerate the madeleines for about 15 minutes to
set. Let come to room temperature before serving.

WHITE CHOCOLATE–PRETZEL COOKIES

makes 12 cookies

....

Another iconic maman cookie, these buttery, golden beauties combine crispy, crunchy pretzels with rich and smooth white chocolate to hit all the right sweet and salty notes. We like to use chocolate baking wafers in our cookies because, unlike chips, they melt into the dough, guaranteeing an extra-gooey center that we're pretty sure will make you fall head over heels. Our favorite way to enjoy these cookies is warm from the oven with a cold glass of milk.

1½ sticks (6 ounces / *170 g*) unsalted butter, at room temperature

1¼ cups (*250 g*) sugar

¼ teaspoon fine sea salt

2 large eggs

½ teaspoon pure vanilla extract

2 cups (*290 g*) all-purpose flour

1 cup (*145 g*) white chocolate baking wafers (such as Guittard)

1 cup (about *50 g*) salted mini pretzels, roughly chopped, plus whole mini pretzels for garnish

notes

1. Set a rack in the center of the oven and preheat to 350°F (*180°C*). Line two sheet pans with parchment paper.

2. In a stand mixer fitted with the paddle attachment, combine the butter, sugar, and salt and beat on medium, scraping down the sides of the bowl as needed, for about 2 minutes to fully combine. Add the eggs, 1 at a time, scraping down the sides of the bowl after each addition and mixing until the dough starts sticking to the sides of the bowl, about 3 minutes total. Add the vanilla and mix for a few seconds to incorporate. Add the flour in 2 batches and mix on low just until no flour is visible, about 1 minute. Add the baking wafers and the roughly chopped pretzels and fold with a wooden spoon for about 30 seconds to evenly distribute.

3. Scoop the dough into roughly ¼-cup (*75 g*) portions and using your hands, roll each portion into a ball (see Tip, page 160). Arrange the balls of dough on the prepared sheet pans, spacing them about 1½ inches (*3.75 cm*) apart. Top each ball of dough with a pretzel, pressing firmly to flatten the cookie slightly.

4. Transfer one sheet pan to the oven and bake, rotating the sheet pan as needed for even baking (see Tip, page 150), until the bottoms and edges are browned but the centers are still a little gooey, 18 to 20 minutes. Let cool on the sheet pan for at least 10 minutes, then enjoy right away or transfer to a wire rack and let cool completely, about 20 minutes. Repeat to bake the remaining cookies.

TIP: *Store the cookies at room temperature in an airtight container for up to 2 days.*

CRUMPET'S DOG COOKIES

makes about 48 dog cookies

Maman is best known for cookies, so we certainly couldn't leave out Crumpet, our beloved four-legged friend. We adopted Crumpet, a mixed-breed dog found abandoned in North Carolina, and named him in honor of the fact that we baked crumpets together on our third date. As a beloved member of our family, Crumpet enjoys homemade meals and treats, including these for-dogs-only cookies, that don't have any of the artificial ingredients found in store-bought dog food. Chocolate is particularly dangerous for dogs, but they can safely enjoy carob chips. The best thing about these cookies is that even if they aren't perfect, your pooch will still love them. This recipe makes a lot, but if your pet is anything like Crumpet, they won't last long!

¾ cup (*180 g*) all-natural, sugar-free, unsalted peanut butter

¼ cup (*60 ml*) vegetable oil

1 large egg

2¼ cups (*326 g*) all-purpose flour

¾ cup (*50 g*) wheat germ (see Tip)

¾ cup (*130 g*) carob chips

1. Preheat the oven to 350°F (*180°C*). Line two sheet pans with parchment paper.

2. In a stand mixer fitted with the paddle attachment, combine the peanut butter, vegetable oil, and egg and mix on low for about 3 minutes to fully combine. Add the flour, wheat germ, and carob chips and mix on low for about 1 minute to fully combine. With the mixer running on low, slowly add ¾ cup (*180 ml*) water and mix until a smooth dough forms.

3. Turn out the dough onto a lightly floured work surface. Using a rolling pin, roll out the dough to about a ½-inch (*1.25 cm*) thickness. Using your favorite cookie cutters (2-inch / *5 cm* cutters will yield about 48 cookies), cut the dough into shapes.

4. Arrange the cookies on the prepared sheet pans and bake until browned around the edges and firm to the touch, 30 to 35 minutes. Turn off the oven and let the cookies stand inside for 1 to 2 hours to dry out and harden.

TIPS:

Wheat germ is a source of omega-3 fatty acids, which will help support your pup's immune system and give them a shiny coat!

Store cookies at room temperature in an airtight container for up to 2 weeks.

notes

cakes and sweet tarts

"My maman is an amazing cook who always created beautiful celebrations—a tradition I'm trying to pass on to my daughters. Whether we're baking pies at Thanksgiving or cupcakes for a bake sale, the important thing is making those memories together."

—DARCY MILLER,
author, illustrator, celebrations expert,
and founder of Darcy Miller Designs

PISTACHIO LOAF CAKE

makes one 9×5-inch (23×12.5 cm) loaf

....

This rich, pale green loaf is one of maman's oldest recipes and a favorite of Ben's family. Pistachio butter infuses the cake with subtle nuttiness without any of the artificial flavors typical of pistachio desserts. Be careful with the green food coloring—a little goes a long way. We serve this pretty loaf upside down, so it has a flat top that we find both unexpected and attractive. It's lovely for breakfast, with tea, or as dessert. It can even be made into a naked cake (see page 183).

CAKE

Vegetable oil spray and flour, for the pan

5 large eggs, separated

2 tablespoons whole milk

2 tablespoons granulated sugar

2½ sticks (10 ounces / *280 g*) unsalted butter, at room temperature

2 cups (*260 g*) confectioners' sugar

1⅔ cups (*175 g*) superfine almond flour

⅓ cup (*80 g*) unsweetened pistachio butter (see Tip, page 172)

⅔ cup (*90 g*) all-purpose flour

Chopped toasted unsalted pistachios

GLAZE

6 ounces (*170 g*) white chocolate, chopped, or 1⅓ cups (*170 g*) white chocolate chips

2 teaspoons canola oil

Green food coloring

notes

....

....

....

....

....

1. **MAKE THE CAKE:** Set a rack in the center of the oven and preheat to 325°F (*163°C*). Coat a 9 × 5-inch (*23 × 12.5 cm*) loaf pan with vegetable oil spray and dust with flour.

2. In a small bowl, whisk together the egg yolks and milk.

3. In a stand mixer fitted with the whisk attachment, whip the egg whites on medium until frothy and doubled in volume, 7 to 10 minutes. With the mixer running on medium-high, add the granulated sugar, 1 tablespoon at a time, and continue whipping until the egg whites are glossy and hold stiff peaks, 3 to 5 minutes. Carefully transfer to a large bowl.

4. In the clean bowl of a stand mixer fitted with the paddle attachment, combine the butter and confectioners' sugar and mix on low, scraping down the sides of the bowl as needed, for about 3 minutes to fully combine. Add the almond flour and pistachio butter and mix on low for about 1 minute to combine. With the mixer still running on low, gradually add the egg yolk mixture and mix, scraping down the sides of the bowl as needed, until fully incorporated, about 1 minute.

5. Using a spatula, gently fold about one-third of the whipped egg whites into the batter until just combined. Add another one-third of the whipped egg whites and half of the all-purpose flour and fold until just combined. Add the remaining whipped egg whites and all-purpose flour and gently fold until no streaks remain, being careful not to overmix the batter.

6. Transfer the batter to the prepared pan. Bake until a toothpick inserted in the center comes out clean, about 1 hour 15 minutes.

RECIPE CONTINUES

TIP: *Pistachio butter is available in some specialty shops or online—we prefer NutRaw because it's made with a touch of salt and vanilla that really rounds out the flavors of this cake— but you can make your own. Pulse 2 cups (280 g) raw unsalted pistachios with a pinch of salt in a food processor until finely chopped, then blend on low, scraping down as needed, until a butter starts to form. Increase the speed to medium and blend until completely smooth. It keeps at room temperature in an airtight container for up to 1 day.*

7. Set a wire rack inside a sheet pan. Set the loaf pan on the wire rack and let cool for 20 minutes, then invert the cake onto the rack and let cool completely, about 1½ hours. Don't flip the cake back over—you want the flat side to be facing up—but if the cake doesn't sit flat, trim the top to make it even.

8. **MEANWHILE, MAKE THE GLAZE:** In a double boiler, or in a heatproof bowl set over a pan of simmering water, melt the white chocolate, stirring as needed. (Alternatively, place the white chocolate in a microwave-safe bowl and microwave in 30-second intervals, stirring after each interval, until fully melted.)

9. Stir the canola oil into the white chocolate, then add green food coloring, 1 drop at a time, until your desired color is reached. Pour the glaze over the cake and use an offset spatula to gently push the glaze so it spills over and covers the sides. Sprinkle the top with pistachios and refrigerate for at least 30 minutes before serving.

CHAMPAGNE CAKE
WITH CRÈME FRAÎCHE AND STRAWBERRIES

makes one 6-inch (15 cm) four-layer cake

....

An iconic French wine, Champagne is one of our drinks of choice, so we love to find ways to enjoy it beyond simply drinking. This unique cake, decorated in maman's signature naked style, is lovely for birthdays and other celebrations. The combination of strawberries and Champagne feels instantly festive, and the sparkling wine helps to soften the cake. It's important to open the Champagne at the last minute to maximize the bubbles. The recipe doesn't use a whole bottle, which means you can enjoy a few glasses while you bake.

CHAMPAGNE CAKE

Vegetable oil spray

2⅔ cups (380 g) all-purpose flour

1½ cups (300 g) granulated sugar

2 teaspoons baking powder

1 teaspoon baking soda

1 teaspoon fine sea salt

3 large eggs

1½ sticks (6 ounces / 170 g) unsalted butter, melted

1½ cups (360 ml) Champagne

CRÈME FRAÎCHE FROSTING

9 ounces (252 g) crème fraîche

9 ounces (252 g) mascarpone

½ cup (65 g) confectioners' sugar

ASSEMBLY

8 ounces (225 g) strawberries, some halved and some sliced

2 ounces (57 g) small edible flowers, such as bachelor's buttons or violas, for garnish (optional)

1. MAKE THE CHAMPAGNE CAKE: Set a rack in the center of the oven and preheat to 350°F (*180°C*). Line the bottom of two 6-inch (*15 cm*) round cake pans with rounds of parchment paper and coat the pans with vegetable oil spray.

2. In a stand mixer fitted with the paddle attachment, combine the flour, granulated sugar, baking powder, baking soda, and salt and mix on low for about 30 seconds to combine. With the mixer running on low, add the eggs, 1 at a time, scraping down the sides of the bowl and mixing until the eggs are fully incorporated after each addition, about 4 minutes total. Add the melted butter and mix for about 30 seconds to fully incorporate. Scrape down the sides of the bowl and mix for 30 seconds more. Add the Champagne and mix on low until a smooth batter forms, about 1 minute.

3. Divide the batter between the prepared pans and bake until a toothpick inserted in the center of each cake comes out mostly clean (a few moist streaks may remain), 45 to 50 minutes.

4. Set the cake pans on a wire rack and let cool in the pans for 30 minutes. Carefully cut around the edges of the cakes to loosen them from the pans, then invert them onto the rack, remove the pans, and let cool completely, about 1½ hours.

5. MEANWHILE, MAKE THE CRÈME FRAÎCHE FROSTING: Place the crème fraîche and mascarpone in a stand mixer fitted with the whisk attachment. With the mixer running on medium, gradually add the confectioners' sugar. When it has all been added, increase the speed to high and whip until the frosting is stiff, about 1 minute.

RECIPE CONTINUES

6. ASSEMBLE THE CAKE: Using a serrated knife, slice the rounded tops off each cooled cake, so they are level and both the same height. Gently dust off any crumbs and discard the tops. Slice each cake horizontally in half to create a total of 4 thin layers.

7. Use a dollop of frosting to secure one of the cake layers to a cake stand. Use an offset spatula to spread about one-quarter of the frosting evenly over the entire top surface of the cake layer, spreading it all the way to the edges, but not going over the sides. Repeat to add two more cake layers, using about one-quarter of the frosting each time. Top with the last cake layer, then spread the remaining frosting evenly over the top.

8. Gently push the strawberry halves and slices into the frosting on top of the cake. Sprinkle with edible flowers (if using).

TIP: *Store the cake refrigerated and covered for up to 3 days.*

notes

ASHLEIGH'S CARROT CAKE
WITH BROWN SUGAR-CREAM CHEESE FROSTING

makes one 9×13-inch (23×33 cm) cake

....

Elisa's maman, Janice, didn't like her daughters eating store-bought sweets, so when they fell in love with a local bakery's carrot cake, she created her own version to best it. Wonderfully moist, deeply spiced, and topped with a brown sugar-cream cheese frosting, Janice's cake immediately won over the Marshall family and has been an Easter tradition ever since. She used to bake it in bunny shapes and let Elisa and her sister, Ashleigh, decorate it with their favorite candies. Canned crushed pineapple is the secret to the cake's moist and tender crumb. And you must use freshly grated carrot—pregrated carrots are far too dry and lack flavor.

CARROT CAKE

Vegetable oil spray

2¼ cups (326 g) all-purpose flour

2 teaspoons baking powder

1 teaspoon baking soda

1 teaspoon fine sea salt

½ teaspoon ground allspice

½ teaspoon ground cardamom

½ teaspoon ground cinnamon

½ teaspoon ground ginger

½ teaspoon grated nutmeg

1½ cups (260 g) packed light brown sugar

1 cup (240 ml) extra-virgin olive oil

4 large eggs

2 cups (220 g) coarsely grated carrots (about 3 large carrots)

1 cup (225 g) drained canned crushed pineapple

1 cup (125 g) chopped raw unsalted walnuts

¾ cup (110 g) raisins (optional)

notes

_____

_____

_____

_____

1. **MAKE THE CARROT CAKE:** Set a rack in the center of the oven and preheat to 325°F (163°C). Coat a 9 × 13-inch (23 × 33 cm) glass baking dish with vegetable oil spray.

2. In a medium bowl, whisk together the flour, baking powder, baking soda, salt, allspice, cardamom, cinnamon, ginger, and nutmeg.

3. In a stand mixer fitted with the paddle attachment, combine the brown sugar, olive oil, and eggs and mix on low for about 3 minutes to fully combine. Add the flour mixture in 3 batches and beat on medium, scraping down the sides of the bowl as needed, until fully combined and smooth after each addition, about 2 minutes total.

4. Fold in the carrots, pineapple, walnuts, and raisins (if using). Transfer the batter to the prepared baking dish. Bake until a toothpick inserted in the center comes out clean, 30 to 35 minutes. Set the dish on a wire rack to cool completely, about 1½ hours.

5. **MEANWHILE, MAKE THE BROWN SUGAR–CREAM CHEESE FROSTING:** In the clean bowl of a stand mixer fitted with the paddle attachment, beat together the cream cheese and butter on high until smooth, creamy, and fully combined, about 3 minutes. Add the brown sugar, vanilla, and salt and mix on low until the brown sugar is fully incorporated, about 30 seconds. With the mixer running on low, gradually add the confectioners' sugar and mix, scraping down the sides of the bowl as needed, until fully incorporated, about 1 minute. Increase the speed to high and beat until soft peaks form, about 2 minutes.

6. Spread the frosting evenly across the top of the cake. Slice and serve.

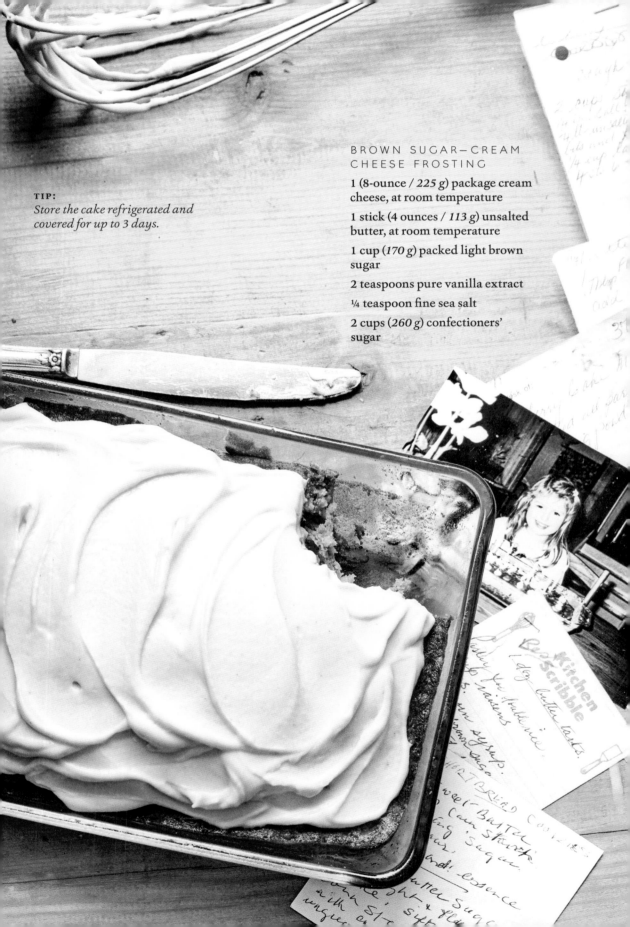

TIP:
Store the cake refrigerated and covered for up to 3 days.

BROWN SUGAR–CREAM CHEESE FROSTING

1 (8-ounce / *225 g*) package cream cheese, at room temperature

1 stick (4 ounces / *113 g*) unsalted butter, at room temperature

1 cup (*170 g*) packed light brown sugar

2 teaspoons pure vanilla extract

¼ teaspoon fine sea salt

2 cups (*260 g*) confectioners' sugar

MANDARIN ORANGE CHOCOLATE CHEESECAKE
makes one 9 ½-inch (24 cm) cheesecake

....

Elisa's maman, Janice, has been collecting recipes for years and has binders full of magazine and newspaper clippings, scribbled with her notes and revisions. She loves chocolate with orange, and tries any recipe she finds featuring this classic combination. Though she changed the recipe to make it her own, the original inspiration for this cheesecake came from a recipe included with a baking pan Janice bought. As a young baker, Elisa loved to help her maman make this dessert, and it remains a family favorite—it's even at the top of Ben's list. Fresh fruit is usually our go-to, but canned mandarin oranges work best here. And while low-fat cream cheese may be tempting, for cheesecake, full-fat is the only way to go.

CHOCOLATE COOKIE CRUST

1¾ cups (*180 g*) chocolate cookie crumbs

¼ cup (*50 g*) sugar

1 teaspoon fine sea salt

1½ sticks (6 ounces / *170 g*) unsalted butter, melted

CHEESECAKE

4 (8-ounce / *225 g*) packages full-fat cream cheese, at room temperature

1½ cups (*300 g*) sugar

3 tablespoons all-purpose flour

2 teaspoons grated orange zest

½ teaspoon pure vanilla extract

4 large eggs

2 large egg yolks

1¼ cups (*180 g*) drained canned mandarin orange segments (see Tip)

6 ounces (*170 g*) semisweet chocolate, chopped, or 1 cup (*170 g*) semisweet chocolate chips

notes

_____

_____

_____

_____

1. **MAKE THE CHOCOLATE COOKIE CRUST:** In a medium bowl, whisk together the chocolate cookie crumbs, sugar, and salt. Add the melted butter and stir until the crumbs are evenly moist. Using your fingers or the back of a spoon, press the cookie mixture into the bottom and up the sides of a 9½-inch (*24 cm*) springform pan, leaving a 1-inch (*2.5 cm*) space at the top. Place in the freezer to set while you make the filling.

2. Set a rack in the center of the oven and preheat to 500°F (*260°C*). If possible, turn on the oven light so you can monitor the cheesecake without opening the door.

3. **MAKE THE CHEESECAKE:** In a stand mixer fitted with the paddle attachment, combine the cream cheese, sugar, flour, orange zest, and vanilla and beat on medium-low until smooth, about 3 minutes. With the mixer running on low, add the whole eggs and egg yolks, 1 at a time, scraping down the sides of the bowl and mixing until the eggs and yolks are fully incorporated after each addition, about 5 minutes total. Fold in 1 cup (*144 g*) of the mandarin orange segments.

4. Place the crust-lined springform pan on a sheet pan. Pour in the cheesecake filling, being sure the crust is completely covered and that some of the filling is above the top of the crust. Bake until the top is puffed, about 5 minutes, checking it every minute to make sure it's not browning too much. Reduce the oven temperature to 200°F (*100°C*) and open the oven door for about 30 seconds to release heat quickly, then continue baking until the cheesecake is mostly firm and jiggles only slightly in the center when the pan is lightly shaken, 50 minutes to 1 hour.

5. Set the cheesecake on a wire rack, carefully run a knife around the edges to loosen it from the sides of the pan (but leave the sides on), and let cool completely. Remove the sides of the springform pan and refrigerate for at least 2 hours and up to 5 days.

6. When ready to serve, in a double boiler or in a heatproof bowl set over a pan of simmering water, melt the chocolate, stirring as needed. (Alternatively, place the chocolate in a microwave-safe bowl and microwave in 30-second intervals, stirring after each interval, until fully melted.)

7. Dip a spoon in the melted chocolate and drizzle it over the cheesecake in a zigzag pattern. Arrange the remaining ¼ cup (*36 g*) orange segments across the top of the cheesecake. Let the cheesecake sit at room temperature for about 30 minutes to set the chocolate, then cut into slices and serve.

TIPS:
This cheesecake can be easily adapted to other flavors. Sometimes we swap raspberries for the mandarin oranges, or skip the oranges and zest and stir in chopped Oreo cookies instead.

Store the cheesecake refrigerated and covered for up to 1 week.

WHITE CHOCOLATE, BLUEBERRY, AND LAVENDER NAKED CAKE

makes one 9-inch (23 cm) three-layer cake

....

This gorgeous cake is pure maman. White chocolate, blueberry, and lavender make for an unexpected and sophisticated flavor combination, while the naked cake look is a maman signature and one of our most frequent requests for showers, weddings, and birthdays—it makes a beautiful centerpiece for any celebration. We also make a simple loaf version at all our locations for daily indulgences. We tried to take it off the menu once and there was such an uproar from our customers that it earned a permanent spot in our pastry case. The recipe takes you through the basics of building a naked cake, but remember that decorating is about creating your own unique cake and that putting your special spin on it is half the fun.

CAKE

Vegetable oil spray

1 cup (*240 ml*) whole milk

¾ cup (*30 g*) dried lavender flowers (see Tip, page 189)

8 large eggs, separated

¼ cup (*50 g*) granulated sugar

4 sticks (1 pound / *450 g*) unsalted butter, at room temperature

3 cups (*390 g*) confectioners' sugar

2⅓ cups (*240 g*) superfine almond flour

1⅓ cups (*190 g*) all-purpose flour

2½ cups (*380 g*) blueberries

FROSTING

4½ ounces (*126 g*) white chocolate, chopped, or 1 cup (*126 g*) white chocolate chips

2 sticks (8 ounces / *225 g*) unsalted butter, at room temperature

4 cups (*520 g*) confectioners' sugar

1 teaspoon pure vanilla extract

ASSEMBLY

Blueberries, for garnish

Dried lavender flowers (see Tip, page 189), for garnish

1. **MAKE THE CAKE:** Set a rack in the center of the oven and preheat to 325°F (*163°C*). Coat three 9-inch (*23 cm*) round cake pans with vegetable oil spray and line the bottoms with rounds of parchment paper.

2. In a small saucepan, bring the milk and dried lavender flowers to a boil over medium heat, keeping a close eye. Remove the pan from the heat and let cool to room temperature, then strain out and discard the lavender.

3. In a stand mixer fitted with the whisk attachment, whip the egg whites on medium-high until frothy and doubled in volume, 5 to 8 minutes. With the mixer still running on medium-high, add the granulated sugar, 1 tablespoon at a time, and continue whipping until the egg whites are glossy and hold stiff peaks, 3 to 5 minutes. Carefully transfer to a large bowl.

4. In the clean bowl of a stand mixer fitted with the paddle attachment, combine the butter and confectioners' sugar and mix on low, scraping down the sides of the bowl as needed, for about 3 minutes to fully combine. Add the almond flour and mix on low until fully incorporated, about 1 minute. With the mixer running on low, add the egg yolks and continue mixing, scraping down the sides of the bowl as needed, until fully incorporated, about 1 minute. With the mixer still running on low, add the lavender-infused milk and continue mixing until fully incorporated, about 1 minute.

5. Using a spatula, gently fold about one-third of the whipped egg whites into the batter until just

RECIPE CONTINUES

combined. Add another one-third of the whipped egg whites and half of the all-purpose flour and fold until just combined. Add the remaining whipped egg whites and all-purpose flour, along with the blueberries, and gently fold until no streaks remain, being careful not to overmix the batter.

6. Divide the batter evenly among the prepared pans and bake until a toothpick inserted in the center of each comes out clean and the cakes start to pull away from the sides of the pan, about 30 minutes.

7. Set the cake pans on wire racks and let the cakes cool for 15 minutes in the pans, then invert onto the racks, remove the pans, and let cool completely (flat-side up), about 1½ hours.

8. **MEANWHILE, MAKE THE FROSTING:** In a double boiler, or in a heatproof bowl set over a pan of simmering water, melt the white chocolate, stirring as needed. (Alternatively, place the white chocolate in a microwave-safe bowl and microwave in 30-second intervals, stirring after each interval, until fully melted.)

9. In the clean bowl of a stand mixer fitted with the paddle attachment, combine the butter and 1 cup (*130 g*) of the confectioners' sugar and mix on low until fully combined, about 1 minute. Continue adding the confectioners' sugar, 1 cup (*130 g*) at a time, and mix on low until fully combined, about 1 minute. Increase the speed to medium and beat until white and very smooth, about 5 minutes. With the mixer running on low, gradually add

the melted white chocolate, followed by the vanilla, and mix, scraping down the sides of the bowl as needed, until fully combined, about 3 minutes. Transfer to a piping bag fitted with a medium round pastry tip. Alternatively, spoon into a resealable plastic bag and snip off a bottom corner.

10. **ASSEMBLE THE CAKE:** Using a serrated knife, slice the rounded tops off each cooled cake, so they are level and all the same height. Gently dust off any crumbs and discard the tops.

11. Use a dollop of frosting to secure one of the cake layers on a cake stand. Pipe about one-quarter of the frosting onto the top of the cake and use an offset spatula to spread it all the way to the edges but not over the sides. Arrange a second cake layer on top of the frosting and top with another one-quarter of the frosting, again spreading it all the way to the edges but not over the sides. Top with the third cake layer and spread the remaining frosting evenly on the top and sides of the cake. Clean off the offset spatula and use it to scrape some of the frosting off the sides of the cake to create the "naked" effect. Decorate the top of the cake with blueberries and dried lavender flowers and serve.

TIP:
Store the cake refrigerated and covered for up to 3 days.

CLASSIC SHORTBREAD DOUGH

Makes enough for three 9½-inch (24 cm) round tart shells
or six 4-inch (10 cm) round tartlet shells

....

This rich dough is a delicious alternative to the dough we use to make quiche (see page 79), and can be used for sweet tarts and pies or as the base for bars and cheesecakes. It's more tender and less delicate, and many people find it far easier to make.

6 sticks (1½ pounds / *675 g*) unsalted butter, at room temperature

1½ cups (*195 g*) confectioners' sugar

1 tablespoon pure vanilla extract

5¼ cups (*760 g*) all-purpose flour

1 tablespoon fine sea salt

Vegetable oil spray

notes

1. In a stand mixer fitted with the paddle attachment, combine the butter and confectioners' sugar and mix on low, scraping down the sides of the bowl as needed, for about 3 minutes to fully combine. Add the vanilla and mix on low until fully incorporated, about 1 minute. Add the flour and salt and mix on low until fully incorporated, 1 to 2 minutes.

2. Turn out the dough onto a lightly floured surface and divide into 3 equal portions. Shape each portion into a tight round disk and wrap in plastic wrap. Refrigerate the dough for at least 1 hour before using (see Tip, page 186).

3. Set a rack in the center of the oven and preheat to 350°F (*180°C*).

4. **TO BAKE A ROUND PLAIN TART SHELL:** Coat a 9½-inch (*24 cm*) round plain tart pan with vegetable oil spray and line a sheet pan with parchment paper.

TO MAKE A SCALLOPED TART SHELL: Coat a 9½-inch (*24 cm*) scalloped tart pan with vegetable oil spray and line a sheet pan with parchment paper.

5. **FOR BOTH:** On a lightly floured surface, use a rolling pin to roll 1 disk of dough into a 12-inch (*30 cm*) round. Carefully roll the dough around the rolling pin, brushing off any excess flour. Unroll the dough over the prepared tart pan and gently tuck it into the edges, using a floured finger to press the dough into each curve and letting excess dough fall over the edge. Roll the rolling pin across the top of the tart pan to cut the dough around the edges, then gently pull the excess dough away to leave a clean edge. Freeze for at least 15 minutes.

6. Remove the tart shell from the freezer, set it on the prepared sheet pan, and generously poke the bottom all over with a fork. Carefully line the tart shell with parchment paper, covering the edges to

RECIPE CONTINUES

TIP: *Store dough tightly wrapped in plastic wrap and refrigerated for up to 1 week or frozen for up to 1 month. If the dough is refrigerated for longer than 1 hour, let it stand at room temperature for about 15 minutes before rolling. If frozen, thaw overnight in the refrigerator before rolling. The tart shells can also be well wrapped and frozen for up to 1 month; use straight from the freezer without thawing.*

notes

prevent burning, then fill with enough pie weights or dried beans to completely cover the surface and weigh down the dough.

7. Bake for 20 minutes, then remove the pie weights and discard the parchment. Bake the empty tart shell until baked through and golden brown, about 8 minutes more. Set the tart pan on a wire rack and let cool completely. The tart shell can be used right away or wrapped in plastic wrap and stored at room temperature overnight.

TO BAKE SIX 4-INCH (10 CM) ROUND TARTLET SHELLS:

1. Follow steps 1 to 3 from page 185, then coat six 4-inch (*10* cm) round tartlet pans with vegetable oil spray and line a sheet pan with parchment paper.

2. On a lightly floured surface, use a rolling pin to roll 1 disk of dough into a 12-inch (*30 cm*) round. Use a knife to cut out six 4½-inch (*11.25 cm*) rounds. Gently press each round of dough into a tartlet pan, then use the knife to scrape off any excess from the tops. Freeze for at least 15 minutes.

3. Remove the tartlet shells from the freezer, set them on the parchment-lined sheet pan, and poke the bottoms generously with a fork. Carefully line the tartlet shells with parchment paper, covering the edges to prevent burning, then fill with pie weights or dried beans to completely cover the surface and weigh down the dough.

4. Bake for 15 minutes, then remove the pie weights and discard the parchment. Bake the empty tartlet shells until baked through and golden brown, about 8 minutes more. Set the tartlet shells on a wire rack and let cool completely. The tartlet shells can be used right away or wrapped tightly in plastic wrap and stored at room temperature overnight.

LAVENDER HOT CHOCOLATE TART
WITH CHOCOLATE SHORTBREAD CRUST

makes one 14×5-inch (35×12.5 cm) tart

Growing up, Ben always looked forward to his family's annual trips to Aix-en-Provence—he was enchanted by the region's fragrant lavender fields. The Sormontes carried home a lot of lavender, which they hung to dry, used in crafts, and, of course, added to recipes. Lavender can taste soapy, but we find that just about everyone enjoys it paired with chocolate, which is why we created this tart, a dessert version of our always-in-demand Lavender Hot Chocolate (page 237). You can also bake this in a 9½-inch (*24 cm*) round plain or scalloped tart pan.

CHOCOLATE SHORTBREAD CRUST

2 sticks (8 ounces / 225 g) unsalted butter, cubed, at room temperature

½ cup (*65 g*) confectioners' sugar

1 teaspoon pure vanilla extract

1¾ cups (*254 g*) all-purpose flour

¼ cup (*20 g*) unsweetened natural cocoa powder

1 teaspoon fine sea salt

CHOCOLATE LAVENDER FILLING

½ cup (*120 ml*) heavy cream

3 large eggs

¾ cup (*150 g*) granulated sugar

3 ounces (*84 g*) dark chocolate baking wafers (such as Guittard)

1 teaspoon pure vanilla extract

1 stick (4 ounces / *113 g*) unsalted butter

2 teaspoons dried lavender powder (see Tip, page 189)

½ teaspoon fine sea salt

LAVENDER WHIPPED CREAM

1 cup (*240 ml*) heavy cream

3 tablespoons confectioners' sugar

½ teaspoon dried lavender powder (see Tip, page 189)

1. MAKE THE CHOCOLATE SHORTBREAD CRUST: In a stand mixer fitted with the paddle attachment, combine the butter, confectioners' sugar, and vanilla and mix on low for about 30 seconds to fully combine. With the mixer running on low, gradually add the flour, cocoa powder, and salt and continue mixing until the cocoa powder is fully incorporated and the dough no longer sticks to the bowl, about 1 minute.

2. Shape the dough into a tight round disk and wrap in plastic wrap. Refrigerate the dough for at least 1 hour before using.

3. Arrange the dough between pieces of parchment paper and use a rolling pin to roll it into a 16 × 7-inch (*40 × 17.5 cm*) rectangle. Carefully roll the dough around the rolling pin, removing the parchment paper. Unroll the dough over a 14 × 5-inch (*35 × 12.5 cm*) rectangular scalloped tart pan and gently tuck it into the edges, using your finger to press the dough into each curve and letting excess dough fall over the edge. Roll the rolling pin across the top of the tart pan to cut the dough around the edges, then gently pull the excess dough away to leave a clean edge. Freeze for at least 15 minutes.

4. Set a rack in the center of the oven and preheat to 350°F (*180°C*). Line a sheet pan with parchment paper.

5. Remove the tart shell from the freezer, set it on the parchment-lined sheet pan, and generously poke the bottom all over with a fork. Carefully line the tart shell with parchment paper, covering the edges to prevent burning, then fill with enough pie weights or dried beans to completely cover the surface and weigh down the dough.

RECIPE AND INGREDIENTS CONTINUE

Whole dried lavender flowers (see Tip)

Shaved dark chocolate

TIPS:

You can buy dried lavender powder in the spice aisle of specialty markets or make your own by grinding dried culinary lavender in a spice grinder—just avoid buying lavender from a florist, which won't be safe to eat. To dry lavender, cut the stems just after the flowers open, then hang the lavender upside down or lay it flat to dry.

When making the chocolate-lavender filling, it's tricky to clip a candy thermometer to the side of a bowl and it won't give you an accurate reading. Instead, just hold an instant-read thermometer in the mixture to determine the temperature.

Store the dough tightly wrapped in plastic wrap and refrigerated for up to 1 week or frozen for up to 1 month. If the dough is refrigerated for longer than 1 hour, let it stand at room temperature for about 15 minutes before rolling. If frozen, thaw overnight in the refrigerator before rolling. Store the tart, covered, in the refrigerator for up to 3 days.

notes

6. Bake for 15 minutes, then remove the pie weights and discard the parchment. Bake the empty tart shell until the bottom no longer looks wet, about 5 minutes more. Set on a wire rack and let cool to room temperature; refrigerate until completely cool.

7. **MAKE THE CHOCOLATE LAVENDER FILLING:** In a stand mixer fitted with the whisk attachment, whip the heavy cream until stiff peaks form, 1 to 2 minutes. Gently scrape into a small bowl and refrigerate.

8. In a medium saucepan, bring 1 cup (*240 ml*) water to a boil. Reduce the heat and let simmer.

9. In a heatproof medium bowl, whisk together the eggs and granulated sugar. Set the bowl over the pan of simmering water and cook, whisking constantly, until the mixture reaches 160°F (*71°C*) on an instant-read thermometer (see Tip). Remove from the heat and very quickly whisk in the baking wafers and vanilla. Let cool for at least 20 minutes.

10. In the clean bowl of a stand mixer fitted with the whisk attachment, combine the butter, dried lavender powder, and salt and whip on medium until the mixture is fluffy and the lavender is fully incorporated, about 1 minute. With the mixer running on low, gradually add the chocolate mixture, then scrape down the sides of the bowl. Whip on high until thick and pale, 2 to 3 minutes. Gently fold in the whipped cream. Pour into the cooled tart shell and refrigerate for at least 30 minutes and up to 1 day to set.

11. **MAKE THE LAVENDER WHIPPED CREAM:** In the clean bowl of a stand mixer fitted with the whisk attachment, whip together the heavy cream, confectioners' sugar, and dried lavender powder on medium until thick, about 1 minute. Scrape down the sides of the bowl, then whip on high until stiff peaks form, about 1 minute more.

12. Gently spread the lavender whipped cream on top of the tart, leaving a small border around the edges. If desired, garnish with whole dried lavender flowers and shaved dark chocolate. Refrigerate for at least 4 hours or overnight to set before serving.

TARTE AU CITRON

makes one 9 ½-inch (24 cm) tart

....

French mamans are judged by their tarte au citron. A proper version must have a sweet buttery crust and be bursting with tart lemon flavor. Our version, inspired by Ben's maman, Joelle, is best served chilled and makes a refreshing summer dessert guaranteed to please lemon lovers. You can dress it up by adding whipped cream—we especially love it piped with a star-shaped pastry tip—a meringue topping, or sprinkling it with lemon slices, lemon zest, toasted almonds, or colorful fresh berries. The curd is incredibly versatile and can be used on pancakes, ice cream, cheesecake, yogurt parfaits, cakes, and in our Lemon Meringue Beignets (page 213).

3 cups (*690 g*) Citron Curd (recipe follows), warm

1 disk Classic Shortbread Dough (page 185) or store-bought, baked in a 9½-inch (*24 cm*) scalloped tart pan and cooled

Whipped cream, lemon slices, and lemon zest, for garnish (optional)

1. Pour the warm citron curd into the cooled tart shell and use an offset spatula to evenly spread it to the edges of the tart shell. Place a piece of plastic wrap directly on the surface of the tart and refrigerate for at least 4 hours or overnight to set.

2. When ready to serve, carefully remove the plastic wrap. Dollop with whipped cream, decorate with lemon slices, and sprinkle with lemon zest, if desired. Enjoy immediately.

CITRON CURD

MAKES ABOUT 3 CUPS (*690 g*)

1¼ cups (*300 ml*) whole milk

1¼ cups (*300 ml*) fresh lemon juice (from about 6 lemons)

5 large egg yolks

½ cup (*100 g*) sugar

⅓ cup (*40 g*) cornstarch

5 tablespoons (*70 g*) unsalted butter, cubed, at room temperature

notes

1. In a medium saucepan, combine the milk and lemon juice. Bring to a boil over medium heat, keeping a close eye.

2. In a medium bowl, whisk together the egg yolks and sugar until fully combined. Add the cornstarch and whisk until fully incorporated. While whisking vigorously, gradually add ¼ cup (*60 ml*) of the hot milk. Repeat with another ¼ cup (*60 ml*) of the hot milk, then slowly add the remaining hot milk, whisking vigorously so the eggs don't scramble.

3. Return the mixture to the saucepan and cook over medium-low heat, whisking constantly, until it's as thick as pudding and bubbling slightly, 3 to 5 minutes. Remove the pan from the heat and whisk vigorously to make sure the curd is smooth, then add the butter pieces, 1 at a time, and whisk until fully incorporated.

MATCHA BLUEBERRY TARTLETS

makes six 4-inch (20 cm) tartlets

....

In addition to our extremely popular matcha beverages—sometimes they outsell our coffee drinks!—we also use matcha in the kitchen. Unlike green tea that you brew and steep, matcha is a stone-ground powder. It's a mood and energy booster, packed with nutrients and antioxidants, and has anti-inflammatory properties. Matcha has grassy notes, a sweet nuttiness, and pleasantly bitter undertones that pair perfectly with sweet, juicy blueberries and our buttery shortbread crust. To add more color and sweeten the flavor, drizzle the tartlets with melted white chocolate.

1¾ cups (*420 ml*) whole milk

4 large egg yolks

½ cup (*100 g*) sugar

3 tablespoons cornstarch

1 tablespoon matcha powder

3 tablespoons unsalted butter, cubed, at room temperature

1 disk Classic Shortbread Dough (page 185), baked in six 4-inch (*10 cm*) tartlet pans and cooled

2 cups (*305 g*) blueberries, for garnish

1. In a medium saucepan, bring the milk to a boil over medium heat, keeping a close eye.

2. In a medium bowl, whisk together the egg yolks and sugar until fully combined. Add the cornstarch and matcha powder and whisk until fully incorporated. While whisking vigorously, gradually add ¼ cup (*60 ml*) of the hot milk. Repeat with another ¼ cup (*60 ml*) of the hot milk, then slowly add the remaining hot milk, whisking vigorously so the eggs don't scramble. Return the mixture to the saucepan and cook over medium-low heat, whisking constantly, until it's as thick as pudding and bubbling slightly, 3 to 5 minutes. Remove the pan from the heat and whisk to make sure the custard is smooth, then add the butter pieces, 1 at a time, and whisk until fully incorporated.

3. Pour the warm custard into the cooled tartlet shells and use an offset spatula to smooth out the tops. Place a piece of plastic wrap directly on the surface of the tartlets and refrigerate for at least 4 hours or overnight to set.

4. When ready to serve, carefully remove the plastic wrap and generously garnish the tartlets with the blueberries. Enjoy immediately.

notes

....
....
....
....
....

*setting a
maman-inspired
table*

In addition to delicious food, maman is known for beautiful table settings, especially our use of vintage blue-and-white tableware. Here are five tips to help you effortlessly achieve a maman-inspired look for your next event or family gathering.

1. DEFY THE RULES Throw out any "rules" you might have heard about table décor and place settings—unless you are hosting the royal family or your uptight grandmother, of course. Instead, have fun and use your imagination. Your friends will appreciate—and remember—your home-cooked food and creative details, not whether or not the water glasses are placed three inches above the knives.

2. MIX AND MATCH In today's modern world, few of us own a set of perfectly matched porcelain, but there's no reason we can't start our own curated collection. As you acquire pieces, try to follow a theme—maman uses blue-and-white florals, for example. If you stick to a common color, pattern, or shape when choosing glassware, plates, and cutlery, your table will be different and unique without looking like it's on display at a garage sale.

3. PLAY WITH TEXTURE Texture is often an afterthought when it comes to setting a table, but playing with raw woods, vintage fabrics, and metallic pops can elevate and add interest to even the simplest of looks. Older-yet-still-lovely handkerchiefs and pieces of lace can double as napkins, placemats, or coasters. They serve the same purpose as new linens, but add a little extra beauty.

4. REPURPOSE AND REUSE Who says teacups are just for tea? Before you look for new items, shop your home first. Cups and saucers can double as dessert or fruit bowls, while vintage glassware and teapots offer unexpected ways to serve hot soup. Many items you own likely have multiple uses, plus you'll get to breathe fresh life into those rarely used, sometimes sentimental pieces.

5. TRY EDIBLE DÉCOR While flowers and foliage are beautiful to look at, edible centerpieces are as much about making an impression as creating an interactive experience for your guests. Charcuterie and cheese platters are staples of the French table, and if you add mini tartines, sandwiches, or quiches, you can create fuller, more eye-catching spreads that are perfect for grazing. For those with a sweet tooth, turn your desserts into a centerpiece. After hours spent in the kitchen, you should relish the beauty of the food you have prepared by setting it on the table to be admired. Some simple florals or berries arranged on or around any sweet treats will enhance them, quickly making them centerpiece-worthy.

TARTES TROPÉZIENNES
makes 12 tropéziennes

....

Also known as la tarte de Saint-Tropez, tarte tropézienne is from Saint-Tropez, where Ben's family often vacationed. It was named by the actress Brigitte Bardot while she was filming *And God Created Woman* in this storied town on the French Riviera. Though it's traditionally made as one large tart—this is Ben's annual birthday cake request—we serve mini versions at maman.

PASTRY CREAM

1 cup (*240 ml*) whole milk

½ vanilla bean, split lengthwise, or 1 tablespoon pure vanilla extract

2 large egg yolks

¼ cup (*50 g*) granulated sugar

3 tablespoons cornstarch

1 tablespoon unsalted butter, cubed, at room temperature

TROPÉZIENNES

Classic Brioche Dough (recipe follows)

1 large egg, beaten

Swedish pearl sugar, for decorating

ORANGE BLOSSOM SYRUP

½ cup (*100 g*) granulated sugar

1 teaspoon orange blossom extract

ASSEMBLY

1 cup (*240 ml*) heavy cream

Confectioners' sugar, for dusting

notes

....

....

....

....

....

....

1. MAKE THE PASTRY CREAM: Place the milk in a medium saucepan and scrape in the vanilla seeds (if using vanilla extract, do not add it yet). Bring to a boil over a medium heat, keeping a close eye.

2. In a medium bowl, whisk together the egg yolks and granulated sugar until fully combined. Add the cornstarch and whisk until fully incorporated. While whisking vigorously, gradually add ¼ cup (*60 ml*) of the hot milk. Repeat with another ¼ cup (*60 ml*) of the hot milk, then slowly add the remaining hot milk, whisking vigorously so the eggs don't scramble. Return the mixture to the saucepan and cook over medium-low heat, whisking constantly, until it's as thick as pudding and bubbling slightly, 3 to 5 minutes. Remove the pan from the heat and whisk vigorously to make sure the pastry cream is smooth, then add the butter, 1 piece at a time, followed by the vanilla extract (if using), and whisk until fully incorporated.

3. Transfer the mixture to a shallow airtight container, place plastic wrap directly on the surface of the cream, and refrigerate overnight or for up to 7 days.

4. MAKE THE TROPÉZIENNES: Line two sheet pans with parchment paper.

5. Divide the dough into 12 equal portions, each weighing about 4 ounces (*113 g*). On a clean work surface, roll each portion into a ball by pushing the dough into the work surface in a circular motion. Arrange the balls of dough evenly on the prepared sheet pans. Cover each sheet pan with a clean kitchen towel and let the dough rise in a warm place until doubled in size, at least 1 hour 30 minutes and up to 2 hours.

RECIPE CONTINUES

6. Preheat the oven to 350°F (*180°C*). Set a wire rack inside a sheet pan.

7. When the balls have doubled in size, use a pastry brush to gently brush them with the beaten egg, then sprinkle pearl sugar generously over the top. Bake until the brioches are golden brown on top and feel hollow inside, 20 to 25 minutes. Transfer to the wire rack and let cool completely, about 30 minutes.

8. **MEANWHILE, MAKE THE ORANGE BLOSSOM SYRUP:** In a small saucepan, combine the granulated sugar and ½ cup (*120 ml*) water and bring to a boil over medium-high heat. Remove the pan from the heat and stir in the orange blossom extract.

9. **ASSEMBLE THE TROPÉZIENNES:** Remove the pastry cream from the refrigerator and whisk until smooth.

10. In a stand mixer fitted with the whisk attachment, whip the heavy cream until stiff peaks form, about 5 minutes. Gently fold one-third of the whipped cream into the pastry cream, followed by another third, and then the remaining third, folding until just combined. If desired, transfer to a piping bag fitted with a large round tip (or, alternatively, spoon into a resealable plastic bag and snip off a bottom corner).

11. Halve each brioche horizontally. Use a pastry brush to gently apply an even layer of the orange blossom syrup on the cut sides. Pipe or use an offset spatula to evenly spread a layer of pastry cream 1 inch (*2.5 cm*) thick across the bottom halves of the brioches. Replace the brioche tops over the cream to close the tropéziennes, dust with confectioners' sugar, and serve.

MAKES ENOUGH FOR 12 BEIGNETS
OR 12 TROPÉZIENNES

Vegetable oil spray

2¼ teaspoons active dry yeast

⅓ cup (*68 g*) plus ½ teaspoon
sugar

⅓ cup (*75 ml*) warm water
(about 100°F / *38°C*)

4 cups (*580 g*) bread flour

1 tablespoon fine sea salt

7 large eggs

1 tablespoon honey

1 tablespoon pure vanilla extract

2½ sticks (10 ounces / *280 g*) cold
unsalted butter, cut into small
pieces

1. Coat a large bowl with vegetable oil spray.

2. Place the yeast and ½ teaspoon of the sugar in a
small bowl, then add the warm water, stir, and let sit for
about 10 minutes, or until foamy. (If the yeast doesn't
foam up, it's not activated, and you'll need to start over
with a new packet.)

3. In a stand mixer fitted with the dough hook
attachment, combine the flour, the remaining ⅓ cup
(*68 g*) sugar, the salt, eggs, honey, vanilla, and yeast
mixture and mix on low until a shaggy dough forms,
about 3 minutes. Increase the speed to medium and
add the butter, 1 piece at a time. Increase the speed
to medium-high and knead until the dough starts to
pull away from the sides of the bowl and passes the
windowpane test (see Tip), 7 to 10 minutes. The dough
will still be sticky. Transfer it to the prepared bowl,
tightly cover the bowl with plastic wrap, and let the
dough rest in the refrigerator for at least 12 hours and
up to 24 hours.

TIP: *To perform the windowpane test, take a piece
of dough the size of a quarter and stretch it without
ripping the dough; if you can almost see through it,
the dough is ready.*

notes

more of our favorites

"Baking with kids can be really stressful, but my maman never lost her cool, always let us crack the eggs and taste the dough, and once the cookies came out of the oven, she'd let us eat as many as we wanted. This experience taught me that sweets are not taboo and gave me a relaxed attitude when baking, which helped make me the baker I am today."

—ERIN MCKENNA,
founder and owner, Erin McKenna's Bakery

PÂTISSERIE MODIFIÉE

As much as we try to bake exactly the right amount, there inevitably are days when we have leftover croissants. But with a little love and creativity, we've found ways to revive those extras so they don't go to waste. For our Almond Croissants, we brush past-their-prime pastries with vanilla syrup and add an almond cream filling. When we have leftover chocolate croissants, we add decadent white chocolate–pistachio cream and crunchy salted pistachios to create our Pistachio-Chocolate Croissants. Lastly, to make our Crème Brûlée Croissants, we use rich pastry cream and crackly caramel brittle to transform flaky plain croissants into a truly decadent treat.

ALMOND CROISSANTS
makes 6 croissants

ALMOND CREAM

1¼ cups (*130 g*) superfine almond flour

1 tablespoon all-purpose flour

1 stick (4 ounces / *113 g*) unsalted butter, at room temperature

½ cup (*100 g*) granulated sugar

2 large eggs

1 teaspoon pure vanilla extract

VANILLA SYRUP

½ cup (*100 g*) granulated sugar

1 teaspoon pure vanilla extract

CROISSANTS

6 large fresh or day-old croissants (about 14 ounces / *400 g*)

Sliced or slivered raw unsalted almonds, for garnish

Confectioners' sugar, for garnish

1. MAKE THE ALMOND CREAM: In a medium bowl, whisk together the almond and all-purpose flours.

2. In a stand mixer fitted with the paddle attachment, beat the butter and granulated sugar on medium-low for about 3 minutes to fully combine. With the mixer running on low, add the eggs, 1 at a time, scraping down the sides of the bowl after each addition and mixing until the eggs are fully incorporated after each addition, about 2 minutes total. Add the vanilla, followed by the flour mixture, and mix on low until fully combined, about 1 minute. Transfer to a piping bag fitted with a medium round pastry tip. (Alternatively, spoon into a resealable plastic bag and snip off a bottom corner.) Refrigerate for at least 4 hours or up to overnight.

3. MAKE THE VANILLA SYRUP: In a small saucepan, combine the granulated sugar and ½ cup (*120 ml*) water and bring to a boil over medium-high heat. Remove the pan from the heat, stir in the vanilla, and let cool for at least 10 minutes.

4. MAKE THE CROISSANTS: Set a rack in the center of the oven and preheat to 350°F (*180°C*). Line a sheet pan with parchment paper.

5. Halve the croissants horizontally, then use a pastry brush to generously apply the vanilla syrup on the cut sides. Pipe a thin layer of almond cream on the bottom half of each croissant, leaving a

RECIPE CONTINUES

1-inch (*2.5 cm*) border around the edges. Replace the croissant tops on the bottoms to close them, then pipe a thin zigzag of almond cream on top. Sprinkle the croissants with enough almonds to cover most of the cream. Place the assembled croissants on the prepared sheet pan.

6. Bake until the tops are golden brown and the cream is fully cooked (the tops won't be easy to lift off the bottoms), about 35 minutes. Transfer to a wire rack and let cool. Dust with confectioners' sugar and enjoy warm or at room temperature.

PISTACHIO-CHOCOLATE CROISSANTS

makes 6 croissants

1 cup (*240 ml*) heavy cream

9 ounces (*252 g*) white chocolate, chopped, or 2 cups (*252 g*) white chocolate chips

3 tablespoons pistachio butter (see Tip, page 172)

6 large fresh or day-old chocolate croissants (about 14 ounces / *400 g*)

Finely chopped toasted salted pistachios, for garnish

1. In a small saucepan, bring the heavy cream to a boil over medium heat, keeping a close eye.

2. Place the white chocolate and pistachio butter in a heatproof medium bowl and pour the hot cream over the top. Let stand for 30 seconds, then whisk vigorously until smooth and thoroughly combined. Place plastic wrap directly on the surface of the pistachio cream and refrigerate to firm up for at least 4 hours or overnight.

3. Halve the croissants horizontally. Transfer the cooled pistachio cream to a piping bag fitted with a medium round pastry tip. (Alternatively, spoon the pistachio cream into a resealable plastic bag and snip off a bottom corner.) Pipe a generous amount of cream onto the bottom half of each croissant, then replace the tops to close. Pipe a generous zigzag of cream on top of each croissant, covering most of the surface, then sprinkle with pistachios and serve.

notes

_____

_____

_____

_____

_____

CRÈME BRÛLÉE CROISSANTS

makes 6 croissants

PASTRY CREAM

2 cups (*480 ml*) whole milk

½ vanilla bean, split lengthwise, or 1 tablespoon pure vanilla extract

4 large egg yolks

⅓ cup (*68 g*) sugar

⅓ cup (*40 g*) cornstarch

3 tablespoons unsalted butter, cubed, at room temperature

CARAMEL BRITTLE

1 cup (*200 g*) sugar

4 tablespoons (2 ounces / *57 g*) unsalted butter, cubed, at room temperature

1 teaspoon fleur de sel

CROISSANTS

6 large fresh or day-old croissants (about 14 ounces / *400 g*)

notes

1. **MAKE THE PASTRY CREAM:** Place the milk in a medium saucepan and scrape in the vanilla seeds (if using vanilla extract, do not add it yet). Bring to a boil over a medium heat, keeping a close eye.

2. In a medium bowl, whisk together the egg yolks and sugar until fully combined. Add the cornstarch and whisk until fully incorporated. While whisking vigorously, gradually add ¼ cup (*60 ml*) of the hot milk. Repeat with another ¼ cup (*60 ml*) of the hot milk, then slowly add the remaining hot milk, whisking vigorously so the eggs don't scramble. Return the mixture to the saucepan and cook over medium-low heat, whisking constantly, until it's as thick as pudding and bubbling slightly, 3 to 5 minutes. Remove the pan from the heat and whisk vigorously to make sure the pastry cream is smooth, then add the butter pieces, 1 at a time, followed by the vanilla extract (if using), and whisk until fully incorporated.

3. Transfer the mixture to a shallow airtight container, place plastic wrap directly on the surface of the cream, and refrigerate overnight or for up to 7 days.

4. **MAKE THE CARAMEL BRITTLE:** Line a sheet pan with parchment paper.

5. In a medium saucepan, whisk the sugar with ¼ cup (*60 ml*) water. Bring to a boil over medium heat. Cook, without stirring, until the sugar just starts to turn reddish brown, about 5 minutes. Immediately remove the pan from the heat and whisk until all the sugar is the same reddish brown color. If the sugar looks too light, return the pan to the heat and cook, whisking constantly. Add the butter and whisk vigorously until fully combined. Whisk in the fleur de sel, then pour the mixture onto the prepared sheet pan and use an offset or silicone spatula to spread into a thin, even layer. Freeze for at least 30 minutes, or until hard.

6. MAKE THE CROISSANTS: Use a metal straw or the wide end of a chopstick to poke holes in both ends and the bottom of each croissant.

7. In a stand mixer fitted with the paddle attachment, mix the pastry cream on low until completely smooth, about 2 minutes. Transfer to a piping bag fitted with a small round pastry tip. (Alternatively, spoon the pastry cream into a resealable plastic bag and snip off a bottom corner—note that this method is a bit messier than using a pastry tip!) Squeeze about ¼ cup (56 g) into each croissant (the holes) until the croissants feel almost full. Pipe more pastry cream in a zigzag on top of each croissant, covering up the holes on the ends.

8. In a food processor, pulse the caramel brittle into fine pieces. (Alternatively, place it in a resealable plastic bag and use a rolling pin to crush it into fine pieces.) Sprinkle the brittle generously over the croissants to cover the pastry cream, and serve.

TIPS:

It's best to use an aged dark rum when baking, but you can substitute rum extract—use 1½ teaspoons for every tablespoon of rum.

Store the canelés at room temperature in an airtight container for up to 3 days, or individually wrapped in plastic wrap in the freezer for up to 1 month. Let come to room temperature before serving.

CANELÉS

makes 12 canelés

....

Canelés are classic French pastry at its finest. Soft, tender, and almost custard-like on the inside with a dark and chewy caramelized crust, canelés are completely unique. This recipe, which comes from our head pastry chef, Jean-Louis Berthet, is surprisingly simple and requires just a handful of basic ingredients. The real secret is time—and patience—as the batter needs to be chilled for at least 24 hours (and longer, if possible). We use a copper canelé mold, but those are expensive. Nonstick molds or ones made of carbon steel are the next best option, followed by silicone versions, though they won't deliver the crisp caramelized exterior that is the mark of proper canelés. Serve these with coffee, tea, or a glass of wine—you won't be able to eat just one!

2 cups (*480 ml*) whole milk

1⅓ cups (*272 g*) sugar

1 tablespoon unsalted butter

1 vanilla bean, split lengthwise

3 large egg yolks

2 tablespoons dark rum (such as Plantation Original Dark Rum; see Tip)

¼ teaspoon fine sea salt

1 cup (*145 g*) all-purpose flour

Vegetable oil spray

1. In a small saucepan, combine the milk, ⅔ cup (*136 g*) of the sugar, and the butter. Scrape in the vanilla seeds and add the pod, too. Bring to a boil over medium-high heat, keeping a close eye.

2. Meanwhile, in a stand mixer fitted with the whisk attachment, whip the egg yolks with the remaining ⅔ cup (*136 g*) sugar, the dark rum, and the salt.

3. When the milk mixture is boiling, discard the vanilla bean pod. With the mixer running on low, slowly add the hot milk and continue whipping until fully combined, 2 to 3 minutes. Gradually add the flour in 4 batches, whipping until fully combined after each addition, about 4 minutes total.

4. Pour the batter through a sieve into a 4-cup (*960 ml*) spouted measuring cup. Cover with plastic wrap and refrigerate for at least 24 hours and up to 48 hours.

5. Set a rack in the center of the oven and preheat to 450°F (*230°C*). Coat a canelé mold with vegetable oil spray and use a pastry brush to make sure all the crevices are covered.

6. Remove the batter from the refrigerator, give it a stir, and fill each canelé mold about three-quarters of the way.

7. Bake for 10 minutes, then reduce the oven temperature to 375°F (*190°C*), rotate as needed for even baking, and continue baking until the tops are golden brown, 30 to 35 minutes. With a small knife, remove each canelé from the pan and set on a wire rack to cool for about 30 minutes.

notes

....

....

....

....

....

....

CHOUQUETTES

makes 24 chouquettes

....

Chouquettes are a traditional French after-school snack—Ben loved them growing up. They are impossibly light and will satisfy the sweetest of sweet tooths thanks to a generous dose of pearl sugar adorning the tops. Pearl sugar can be hard to find in supermarkets but is readily available online. Look for Swedish pearl sugar rather than the Belgian variety, which is larger and only for waffles. Chouquettes are best the day they are baked.

Vegetable oil spray

5 tablespoons (*70 g*) unsalted butter, cubed

2 teaspoons granulated sugar

¼ teaspoon fine sea salt

½ cup (*73 g*) all-purpose flour

2 large eggs

2 tablespoons whole milk, plus more as needed

Swedish pearl sugar, for decorating

notes

1. Set a rack in the center of the oven and preheat to 425°F (*218°C*). Line a sheet pan with parchment paper, then lightly coat the paper with vegetable oil spray.

2. In a medium saucepan, combine the butter, granulated sugar, salt, and ½ cup (*120 ml*) water and bring to a boil over medium heat, keeping a close eye. Remove the pan from the heat, add the flour, and stir vigorously with a wooden spoon until fully incorporated. Return the pan to very low heat and cook, stirring, for about 1 minute, or until the dough seems drier and no longer sticks to the sides of the pan.

3. Transfer the mixture to a stand mixer fitted with the paddle attachment. With the mixer running on low, add the eggs, 1 at a time, scraping down the sides of the bowl after each addition and mixing until the eggs are fully incorporated, about 2 minutes total. Transfer to a piping bag fitted with a medium round pastry tip. (Alternatively, spoon the filling into a resealable plastic bag and snip off a bottom corner.) Pipe 1-inch (*2.5 cm*) rounds of dough, about 1 inch (*2.5 cm*) apart, onto the prepared sheet pan.

4. Using a pastry brush, lightly brush a bit of milk on each chouquette, gently pressing to smooth out any pointy tips that remain from piping. Sprinkle generously with pearl sugar.

5. Transfer to the oven, then immediately reduce the temperature to 375°F (*190°C*) and bake for 12 minutes. Rotate the sheet pan as needed for even baking (see Tip, page 150) and bake until the chouquettes are golden brown on top and feel hollow inside, 7 to 10 minutes more. Let cool on the sheet pan for at least 15 minutes, then serve warm or at room temperature.

LEMON MERINGUE BEIGNETS

makes 12 beignets

This extra-special treat combines two of our favorite desserts—traditional French beignets and our Tarte au Citron (page 190). We use our classic brioche dough to make the doughnuts and fill them with plenty of tangy lemon curd, though you can also use jam or different seasonal fillings. A toasted meringue topping is the crowning jewel; it adds an extra layer of texture and flavor. While our recipe includes directions for toasting the meringue under the broiler, you can use a kitchen blowtorch if you have one. Keep the flame on low and guide it evenly across the meringue until deeply browned.

BEIGNETS

Vegetable oil spray

Classic Brioche Dough (page 199)

1 cup (*200 g*) sugar, for coating

Vegetable oil, for frying

Citron Curd (page 190), chilled

MERINGUE

3 large egg whites

⅔ cup (*136 g*) sugar

¼ teaspoon cream of tartar

¼ teaspoon fine sea salt

notes

1. **MAKE THE BEIGNETS:** Line a sheet pan with parchment paper, then coat the paper with vegetable oil spray.

2. Divide the brioche dough into 12 equal portions, each weighing about 4 ounces (*113 g*). On a clean work surface, roll each portion into a ball by pushing the dough into the work surface in a circular motion. Arrange the balls of dough evenly on the prepared sheet pan. Cover the sheet pan with a clean kitchen towel and let the dough sit in a warm place until doubled in size, 1 hour 30 minutes or up to 2 hours.

3. Place the sugar in a small bowl. Set the sugar and a sheet pan near the stove.

4. Clip a candy thermometer to the side of a large Dutch oven or heavy-bottomed saucepan, fill with about 2 inches (*5 cm*) of vegetable oil, and heat to 300°F (*150°C*) over medium-high heat. Reduce the heat to low, add 3 balls of dough, and fry, adjusting the heat as needed, until dark golden brown on the bottom, about 8 minutes. Flip and fry until dark golden brown all over and cooked through, about 8 minutes more (see Tip, page 214). Using a slotted spoon, remove the beignets from the oil, immediately toss them in the sugar to coat, and place on the sheet pan. Repeat with the remaining dough balls, adjusting the heat as needed to keep the oil at 300°F (*150°C*).

5. Stir the citron curd until smooth, then transfer to a piping bag fitted with a small tip. (Alternatively, spoon the curd into a resealable plastic bag and snip off a bottom corner.) Use a metal straw or the wide end of a chopstick to cut a ¼- to ½-inch (*5 mm*

RECIPE CONTINUES

TIP: *The beignets will be browned after a few minutes in the oil; don't be tempted to take them out early—they need the full 16 minutes in hot oil to cook through.*

to 1.25 cm) hole in the side of each beignet. Pipe in the curd, wiping away any excess, and return to the sheet pan.

6. **MAKE THE MERINGUE:** Set a rack 2 to 4 inches (*5 to 10 cm*) from the oven's heat source and turn the broiler to high.

7. In a stand mixer fitted with the whisk attachment, whip the egg whites on medium until frothy and doubled in volume, 3 to 5 minutes. With the mixer running on medium, gradually add the sugar, followed by the cream of tartar and salt, and whip until the mixture is glossy and holds stiff peaks, 5 to 7 minutes. Transfer to a piping bag fitted with a large tip (or a plastic bag with a corner snipped off) and pipe a generous zigzag of meringue on top of each beignet. (Alternatively, use a spatula to spread a layer of meringue on each beignet and create swoops.)

8. Arrange 6 of the beignets on a sheet pan and broil, rotating the pan for even toasting, until the meringue is just toasted, 30 seconds to 1 minute. Remove from the oven and set aside. Repeat to toast the tops of the remaining beignets and serve immediately.

"DEEP-FRIED" ICE CREAM

WITH CROISSANT CRISPS, CHOCOLATE GANACHE, AND PRALINE CRUNCH

serves 6

This unexpected dessert was created for a special Valentine's Day dinner we hosted at maman Soho. It's inspired by the deep-fried ice cream served at Mexican cantinas, but it has a French twist. We roll scoops of vanilla bean ice cream in the crumbs of toasted and crushed croissants to create the "fried" effect, then serve them with bittersweet chocolate ganache and an irresistible hazelnut praline crunch.

DARK CHOCOLATE GANACHE

4 ounces (*113 g*) bittersweet chocolate, roughly chopped

1 cup (*240 ml*) heavy cream

Fine sea salt

PRALINE CRUNCH

¾ cup (*102 g*) skinned hazelnuts

¼ teaspoon fine sea salt

½ cup (*100 g*) sugar

"DEEP-FRIED" ICE CREAM

1 pint (*437 ml*) vanilla bean ice cream

3 croissants (about 7 ounces / *200 g*), torn

Fine sea salt

notes

1. **MAKE THE DARK CHOCOLATE GANACHE:** Place the chocolate in a heatproof medium bowl. In a small saucepan, heat the heavy cream over medium heat just until bubbles start to form around the edges of the pan, about 1 minute. Pour the hot cream over the chocolate, add a pinch of salt, and whisk until smooth. Refrigerate, stirring occasionally, until cool and thick, about 30 minutes.

2. **MEANWHILE, MAKE THE PRALINE CRUNCH:** Preheat the oven to 350°F (*180°C*). Line a sheet pan with parchment paper.

3. In a food processor, process the hazelnuts until finely chopped. Spread in an even layer on the prepared sheet pan and toast until fragrant and lightly browned, 5 to 7 minutes. In a small bowl, toss ½ cup (*68 g*) of the toasted hazelnuts with the salt; set the remainder aside. Reserve the parchment-lined sheet pan.

4. In a small saucepan, whisk the sugar with 2 tablespoons water. Bring to a boil over medium heat. Cook, without stirring, until the sugar just starts to turn reddish brown, about 5 minutes. Immediately remove the pan from the heat and whisk until all the sugar is the same reddish brown color. If the sugar looks too light, return the pan to the heat and continue to cook, whisking constantly. Add the ½ cup (*68 g*) salted hazelnuts and stir to coat in the sugar, then quickly pour the mixture onto the reserved sheet pan and use an offset or silicone spatula to spread into a thin, even layer. Let cool until brittle and room temperature, about 5 minutes. Break into small pieces.

RECIPE CONTINUES

TIP: *You can prep much of this dessert in advance: Store the ganache refrigerated in an airtight container for up to 5 days; reheat gently in a double boiler or a heatproof bowl set over a pan of simmering water before using. Store the praline crunch at room temperature in an airtight container for up to 1 week.*

5. **MAKE THE "DEEP-FRIED" ICE CREAM:** Preheat the oven to 350°F (*180°C*). Line two sheet pans with parchment paper.

6. Using an ice cream scoop or spoon, scoop 6 balls (about ¼ cup / *55 g* each) of ice cream, keeping them as round and compact as possible, and place 1 inch (*2.5 cm*) apart on one of the prepared sheet pans. Freeze until firm, about 10 minutes.

7. Meanwhile, spread the torn croissants in an even layer on the other sheet pan. Bake, tossing occasionally, until the white insides turn golden brown, 8 to 10 minutes. Let cool slightly, then transfer to a food processor and pulse into chunky crumbs. Transfer to a medium bowl and toss with a pinch of salt.

8. Remove the ice cream balls from the freezer and set up three stations: the ice cream balls, the croissant crisps, and a large plate. Using clean hands, roll an ice cream ball through the croissant crisps, pressing to coat, then gently squeeze and shape the ice cream to form a perfect ball. Roll the ice cream through the crisps a second time, then set on the plate and place in the freezer. Repeat with the remaining ice cream and croissant crisps, returning the ice cream to the freezer as needed if it becomes too soft.

9. **TO SERVE:** Place a dollop of the chocolate ganache on each of six plates, dividing it evenly and spreading it toward the edges. Arrange a "deep-fried" ice cream ball in the center and sprinkle with the praline crunch and the reserved toasted hazelnuts. Stick 2 pieces of praline crunch on top of each ice cream ball. Serve immediately.

VANILLA BEAN RIZ AU LAIT

serves 4

....

Riz au lait, rice with milk, is France's answer to rice pudding. Our version is adapted from one made by our pastry chef Jean-Louis's grandmother. We use light brown sugar to add caramel-like color and flavor, while doubling up on vanilla for a richer, more vanilla-forward result. Use more or less milk to suit your palate—and if you add a little bit too much, simply remove the lid to steam off the extra. Finish with a sprinkle of cardamom or cinnamon, or with a drizzle of dulce de leche. We serve this simple yet sophisticated dessert in vintage blue-and-white cups and saucers.

2 cups (*480 ml*) whole milk, plus more for serving

1 cup (*240 ml*) heavy cream

2 vanilla beans, split lengthwise

1 cup (*200 g*) short-grain white rice, such as Arborio or Carnaroli

½ cup (*90 g*) packed light brown sugar

1 tablespoon pure vanilla extract

Ground cardamom, ground cinnamon, or dulce de leche, for garnish (optional)

1. In a medium saucepan, combine the milk and heavy cream. Scrape in the vanilla seeds and add the pods, too. Bring to a boil over medium heat, keeping a close eye. Add the rice, reduce the heat to low, cover, and simmer, stirring occasionally, until the rice is tender, about 30 minutes.

2. Discard the vanilla pods and add the brown sugar and vanilla extract. Simmer, stirring frequently, until as thick as Greek yogurt, about 10 minutes.

3. Remove the pan from the heat and stir in more milk as desired for a looser consistency. Spoon into small cups or bowls and, if desired, garnish with cardamom, cinnamon, or dulce de leche.

notes

MAMAN'S COOKIE TIRAMISÙ

serves 6

....

Tiramisù—or any coffee-infused sweet—is Elisa's go-to dessert order. To put a fun twist on this Italian classic, we swap the traditional ladyfingers for chunks of our signature nutty chocolate chip cookies. You can use any homemade or store-bought chocolate chip cookies, but if they are particularly sweet, you may need to pull back on the sugar. This tiramisù is ideal for entertaining because it's super simple to prepare and is best made in advance—it actually tastes even better the next day!

2 cups (*480 ml*) heavy cream

2 cups (*480 g*) mascarpone

¼ cup (*50 g*) sugar

1 teaspoon pure vanilla extract

1 cup (*240 ml*) strong brewed espresso, warm (about 6 shots; see Tip)

8 Maman's Nutty Chocolate Chip Cookies (page 151) or store-bought chocolate chip cookies (about 30 ounces / *840 g* total)

2 tablespoons unsweetened natural cocoa powder

notes

1. In a stand mixer fitted with the whisk attachment, whip the heavy cream on high until stiff peaks form, about 3 minutes. Transfer to a medium bowl.

2. In the clean bowl of a stand mixer fitted with the whisk attachment, combine the mascarpone, sugar, and vanilla and whip on high, scraping down the sides of the bowl as needed, until smooth and creamy, about 1 minute. Add the whipped cream and gently fold with a rubber spatula to combine without deflating the mixture.

3. Pour the espresso into a wide, shallow bowl. Set aside half of 1 cookie for garnish. Break 4 of the cookies into large chunks, add them to the espresso, and let soak, flipping once, until saturated but not falling apart, 45 to 60 seconds per side. Reserve the espresso. Arrange the soaked cookies on the bottom of an 8-inch (*20 cm*) square baking pan, pressing down to create an even layer. Spread half of the mascarpone whipped cream evenly on top of the cookies. Using a small fine-mesh sieve, dust 1 tablespoon of the cocoa powder over the mascarpone whipped cream.

4. Soak the remaining cookies in the reserved espresso. Use the soaked cookies, the remaining mascarpone whipped cream, and the remaining cocoa powder to create a second layer. Crumble the reserved half cookie and sprinkle on top of the tiramisù. Cover with plastic wrap and refrigerate for at least 2 hours and up to 5 days. Serve chilled.

TIP: *If you don't have an espresso machine at home, brew a dark-roast coffee or use instant espresso powder. What's important is that you don't forgo the espresso or coffee—its flavor is essential to tiramisù. If you prefer a bolder coffee flavor, sprinkle a little instant espresso powder between the layers.*

BEN'S BRÛLÉE

serves 6

....

Ben loves sweets and cannot resist the contrasting textures that are crème brûlée's signature. This vanilla-infused version, perfected by our former pastry chef Vanessa, is his favorite—and he's tried many! We love to serve it for dinner parties because it's individually portioned—we don't have to cut and plate dessert! If you happen to have a kitchen blowtorch, skip the broiler and use the torch instead to create the caramelized top.

2 cups (*480 ml*) heavy cream

1 vanilla bean, split lengthwise

1 teaspoon pure vanilla extract

3 large egg yolks

½ cup plus 2 tablespoons (*75 g*) sugar

⅛ teaspoon fine sea salt

1. Set a rack in the center of the oven and preheat to 325°F (*163°C*). Arrange six ½-cup (4-ounce / *120 ml*) ramekins in a large baking dish.

2. Pour the cream into a small saucepan. Scrape in the vanilla seeds and add the pod, too. Bring to a boil over medium heat, keeping a close eye. Remove the pan from the heat and whisk in the vanilla extract.

3. Meanwhile, in a teakettle, bring 4 cups (*960 ml*) water to a boil. When the water is boiling, remove the kettle from the heat.

4. In a stand mixer fitted with the whisk attachment, whip the egg yolks, ½ cup (*50 g*) of the sugar, and the salt on medium until pale yellow, about 2 minutes. Discard the vanilla pod from the hot cream. With the mixer running on medium-low, slowly stream in the hot cream, scraping down the sides of the bowl as needed.

5. Divide the mixture evenly among the ramekins, then carefully pour enough of the hot water into the baking dish to come about halfway up the sides of the ramekins—you may not use all of the water.

6. Bake until the crèmes brûlées are set but slightly wobbly in the center, 45 to 50 minutes. Carefully remove the ramekins from the baking dish and let cool for about 30 minutes at room temperature, then refrigerate, covered, for at least 2 hours or overnight.

7. At least 30 minutes before serving, place a rack close to the oven's heat source and set to broil.

8. Sprinkle the remaining 2 tablespoons sugar in a thin, even layer over the crèmes brûlées, tapping out any excess. Broil until the sugar is evenly caramelized, 5 to 8 minutes. Let cool for at least 15 minutes before serving. Crème brûlée can also be served chilled: Let it cool for about 30 minutes, then refrigerate until ready to serve.

notes

_____

_____

_____

_____

_____

drinks

"My kids are always with me in the kitchen, and I hope to pass on to them that food can be simple to make, nourishing, *and* delicious! You really can have it all when it comes to making cleaner choices with food."

—Laurel Gallucci,
cofounder and CEO, Sweet Laurel

café fait-maison
coffee at home

If you love coffee as much as we do, but don't live near a maman location, you can still enjoy a great cup at home. We asked Caitlin, our beverage director, to share her best at-home tips. Caitlin was not only our first employee but also the first person we ever interviewed, so she's been an integral part of the maman family from day one—plus she makes amazing coffee.

Caitlin's advice is simple and will undoubtedly improve your coffee experience no matter the beans or brewing method. Once you master the perfect cup, try experimenting with different syrups, like our Cardamom-Orange Honey Syrup (page 230) or Mocha Syrup (page 230). And remember that the real secret to perfect coffee is that it always tastes best in a pretty cup. At maman, we use vintage cups and saucers and are known for our blue-and-white patterned to-go cups.

BUY WHOLE BEANS. Preground coffee beans will never offer as much depth of flavor as whole beans that are ground right before brewing.

CHECK THE ROAST DATE. For optimal freshness, look for beans that were roasted within the last four weeks. Roasted beans need to rest for at least a week prior to brewing.

STORE BEANS PROPERLY. Beans should be kept in an airtight container at room temperature and out of direct sunlight.

GET A GOOD GRIND. How coarse or fine you grind beans depends on how you brew your coffee. Invest in a grinder with a dial setting to adjust for your coffee brewing method.

TASTE THE WATER. Coffee is 98 percent water, so the quality of the water you use will greatly impact your brew. If your tap water has an unpleasant odor or flavor, try using filtered or experimenting with different bottled options.

TEST THE WATER TEMPERATURE. The ideal temperature for brewing coffee is about 200°F (*100°C*). Colder water won't extract enough flavor from the beans, while hotter water will extract bitter flavors.

PUMPKIN-CHAI SYRUP

makes 2 cups (480 ml)

....

Elisa loves the taste of pumpkin but finds most syrups too sweet and artificial tasting. This homemade version delivers that warm, deeply spiced flavor we all crave come fall, yet it is made with real ingredients, so it's natural and better for you. Enjoy this syrup in a latte or hot coffee, or get creative and drizzle it on crumb cake or a yogurt parfait. For evening, dress it up with bourbon and seltzer served on the rocks, with a cinnamon stick to be extra festive.

1 cup (*240 ml*) boiling water

2 chai tea sachets, or 1 tablespoon loose chai tea in a tea ball

3 tablespoons granulated sugar

3 tablespoons packed light brown sugar

½ teaspoon ground cinnamon

¼ teaspoon ground cloves

⅛ teaspoon grated nutmeg

⅛ teaspoon ground ginger

2 cinnamon sticks

1 cup (*225 g*) canned pure pumpkin puree

1. Pour the boiling water over the tea in a heatproof bowl or cup and steep for at least 5 minutes and no more than 10 minutes, then remove the tea sachet or tea ball.

2. In a medium saucepan, whisk together the granulated sugar, brown sugar, ground cinnamon, cloves, nutmeg, and ginger. Add the cinnamon sticks, pumpkin puree, brewed chai tea, and 1 cup (*240 ml*) water and stir until fully combined. Place over medium heat and cook, whisking occasionally, until gently boiling, 8 to 10 minutes. Reduce the heat to low and cook until reduced by one-quarter and thick enough to coat the back of a wooden spoon, about 15 minutes.

3. Remove the pan from the heat and let cool to room temperature, about 25 minutes. Discard the cinnamon sticks. Store refrigerated in an airtight container for up to 1 month.

notes

....

....

....

....

....

MOCHA SYRUP

makes 1 cup (240 ml)

Although this is really a chocolate syrup, we use it to make mocha lattes at maman, so we've nicknamed it mocha syrup. It's incredibly easy to make and a little goes a long way. In addition to lattes, it can be stirred into your morning coffee or your child's milk or drizzled on ice cream. We've kept the yield small—a cup is enough for about five drinks—because this syrup keeps for only 2 days in the fridge.

1¼ cups (*200 g*) sweetened natural cocoa powder

½ cup (*120 ml*) boiling water

In a small heatproof bowl, combine the cocoa powder and boiling water and whisk until the cocoa powder is fully incorporated and there are no lumps. Store refrigerated in an airtight container for up to 2 days.

CARDAMOM-ORANGE HONEY SYRUP

makes 2 cups (480 ml)

We use this syrup in a latte garnished with candied orange peel. Its citrus notes pair beautifully with espresso, but this syrup is equally at home in hot or iced coffee or tea and makes an amazing spiked dessert, perfect for dinner parties. Simply add a scoop of vanilla ice cream, a shot of whiskey or bourbon, and 2 tablespoons of the syrup to a cup of hot coffee or a shot of espresso, then top with whipped cream and sprinkle with cardamom. We also use this syrup to sweeten our morning oatmeal—it's a brighter, fresher twist on the usual cinnamon sugar.

1 large orange

½ cup (*120 ml*) honey

1 tablespoon ground cardamom

notes

1. Using a vegetable peeler, remove 5 strips of zest from the orange. Juice the orange, measure out ¼ cup (*60 ml*), and reserve any extra for another use. Transfer the juice to a medium saucepan and add the orange zest strips, honey, cardamom, and 2 cups (*480 ml*) water. Set over medium-high heat and stir to dissolve the honey. Bring to a gentle boil, then reduce the heat to low and simmer gently, stirring occasionally, until thick and reduced by about ¼ cup (*60 ml*), 10 to 15 minutes.

2. Remove the pan from the heat and let cool to room temperature. Strain the syrup through a fine-mesh sieve or cheesecloth into an airtight container and discard the orange zest strips. Store refrigerated for up to 1 month.

HONEY-LAVENDER SYRUP

makes 2 cups (480 ml)

Lavender and honey come together beautifully to create a syrup that's slightly sweet, a touch floral, and super comforting. We use it to make our Earl Grey Tea Latte (page 233), but it makes a perfect addition to any hot coffee or tea and can even be added to bubbly—garnish with a sprig of dried lavender to give the drink a bit of extra sparkle! However you use this heavenly syrup, start with about 2 tablespoons and add more to taste.

1⅓ cups (*315 ml*) honey

¾ cup (*20 g*) dried lavender flowers (see Tip, page 189)

2 cups (*480 ml*) boiling water

1. In a heatproof medium bowl, combine the honey, dried lavender flowers, and boiling water and stir until the honey is dissolved and the lavender floats to the top. Let stand for at least 1 hour.

2. Strain the syrup through a fine-mesh sieve or cheesecloth into an airtight container and discard the lavender. Store refrigerated for up to 2 weeks.

notes

EARL GREY TEA LATTE

makes 1 drink

....

The scent of this tea latte brings to mind sweet memories of Ben's grandmother, who drank tea in the morning, afternoon, and after dinner. Adding hot milk and our Honey-Lavender Syrup to Earl Grey tea creates a latte so good even devoted coffee lovers find it hard to resist. Using high-quality tea is especially important—Sloane Tea from Toronto is our go-to source. We like to use whole milk, almond milk, or oat milk, but feel free to use your favorite. And if you have a steamer wand, steam the milk for a richer, creamier latte.

1 cup (*240 ml*) boiling water

**1 Earl Grey tea sachet, or
1½ teaspoons loose Earl Grey tea in a tea ball**

½ cup (*120 ml*) whole milk or any nondairy milk

1 teaspoon Honey-Lavender Syrup (page 231)

Dried lavender flowers (see Tip, page 189), for garnish

1. Pour the boiling water over the tea in a mug and steep for 3 to 5 minutes, depending on your desired strength. Remove the tea sachet or tea ball.

2. Meanwhile, in a small saucepan, combine the milk and honey-lavender syrup and warm, stirring, over low heat until hot to the touch, about 5 minutes.

3. Add the milk mixture to the mug of tea, garnish with dried lavender flowers, and enjoy.

notes

SPICED TURMERIC TEA

makes 3 drinks

....

We originally hired Maddy Gentile, now our operations director, as a barista. She's incredibly passionate about coffee and always seems to have a great new recipe up her sleeve. She created this turmeric tea while looking for more holistic ways to treat the pain she was having from an ankle injury. With powerful anti-inflammatory and antioxidant properties, this brilliant orange root is incredibly healing. Maddy combined it with cinnamon, star anise, allspice, and black pepper to create a deeply spiced drink that tastes fantastic while also delivering an extra boost of care. It's a great way to start or end the day and makes a soothing digestif. Add a squeeze of lemon and a drizzle of honey, if desired.

2 cinnamon sticks

1 whole star anise

2¼ teaspoons allspice berries

½ teaspoon black peppercorns

½ ounce (*14 g*) finely chopped fresh turmeric

1 cup (*240 ml*) hot water

1. In a medium saucepan, combine the cinnamon sticks, star anise, allspice, peppercorns, and 5 cups (*1.2 liters*) water and bring to a boil over high heat. Reduce the heat to medium and simmer for 10 minutes to meld the flavors.

2. In a blender, combine the turmeric and hot water and blend on high until the mixture is thick with no large chunks of turmeric, about 5 seconds. Add to the simmering liquid, then remove the pan from the heat, cover, and let stand for 20 minutes to steep.

3. Strain through a fine-mesh sieve or cheesecloth into an airtight container, discarding any solids. Serve the tea hot or over ice. Store refrigerated for up to 3 days.

notes

LAVENDER HOT CHOCOLATE

makes 2 drinks

....

Lavender is a favorite flavor at maman. We adore the taste and aroma, but it's also a nod to Ben's French heritage. This hot chocolate is one of our most iconic drinks and has brought us a ton of press and many tourists eager to try it. One sip and you'll feel instantly relaxed—and transported to the South of France. Give it an extra kick by adding a double shot of espresso. Or if you like this hot chocolate as much as we do, try our Lavender Hot Chocolate Tart (page 187), which turns this drink into a dessert.

½ cup (*80 g*) natural sweetened cocoa powder (see Tip), plus more for serving (optional)

¼ cup (*60 ml*) hot water

1 tablespoon dried lavender flowers (see Tip, page 189)

2½ cups (*600 ml*) whole milk or any nondairy milk

Marshmallows, for garnish (optional)

1. In a small saucepan, whisk together the cocoa powder, hot water, and dried lavender flowers to create a paste. Add the milk and whisk until fully incorporated. Bring to a simmer over medium heat, stirring occasionally and keeping a close eye.

2. Strain the hot chocolate through a fine-mesh sieve or cheesecloth into mugs and discard the lavender flowers. Add marshmallows (if using), sprinkle with cocoa powder, if desired, and serve.

TIP: *Natural sweetened cocoa powder is also sold as hot cocoa powder or hot chocolate powder, and is not to be confused with regular cocoa powder, which doesn't contain any sugar. Make sure you use one that is made with only cocoa and sugar.*

notes

MAMAN'S NUTTY CHOCOLATE CHIP
HOT CHOCOLATE

makes 2 drinks

....

So many of our customers at maman dunk cookies into their drinks that we thought, Why not combine the two? This decadent hot chocolate is topped with crumbles of our wildly popular nutty chocolate chip cookies. Sure, if you don't have any lying around, you'll have to make a batch of cookies to fully enjoy this drink, but who's ever been sad about making cookies? Walnut milk and oat milk combine to create an especially luscious and silky hot chocolate, but you can use any milk or nondairy alternative you prefer. We find that larger crumbles often sink to the bottom of the drink, a "problem" we've solved by serving additional cookies on the side for dunking.

½ cup (*80 g*) natural sweetened cocoa powder (see Tip, page 237)

¼ cup (*60 ml*) hot water

1½ cups (*360 ml*) unsweetened walnut milk

1½ cups (*360 ml*) unsweetened oat milk

1 Maman's Nutty Chocolate Chip Cookie (page 151) or store-bought, crumbled

1. In a small saucepan, whisk together the cocoa powder and hot water to create a smooth, lump-free paste. Add the walnut milk and oat milk, set over low heat, and whisk for 1 minute to fully incorporate. Increase the heat to medium and bring to a simmer, stirring occasionally and keeping a close eye.

2. Pour into mugs, top with cookie crumbles, and serve.

notes

....
....
....
....
....
....

CINNAMON APPLE CIDER

makes 4 drinks

The pop of apple cider in this drink instantly takes us back to childhood trips to the pumpkin patch. At maman, we add a blend of cinnamon, star anise, and ginger and serve it hot—it's guaranteed to warm you up on the chilliest of days. When entertaining at home, we love to ladle this cider straight from the stove, which has the added benefit of filling the house with the most comforting aroma. To make it more of a party cider, add a few shots of rum or brandy, and for a more gingery drink, use chopped peeled fresh ginger.

6 cups (*1.4 liters*) apple cider

8 cinnamon sticks

2 whole star anise

1 teaspoon ground cinnamon, plus more for serving

½ teaspoon ground ginger

1. In a small saucepan, heat the apple cider over low heat until slightly warm, about 5 minutes. Add 4 of the cinnamon sticks, the star anise, ground cinnamon, and ginger and stir to combine. Increase the heat to medium-high and bring to a gentle boil, then reduce the heat to low.

2. Ladle into mugs or glasses straight from the pan. Garnish with cinnamon sticks and a sprinkle of cinnamon.

notes

ROSE AND ELDERFLOWER LEMONADE

makes 6 drinks

....

This lemonade is our go-to bridal or baby shower mocktail, as well as our go-to shower *cocktail* when spiked with vodka and St-Germain elderflower liqueur. Rose and elderflower bring subtle fruity, floral notes without tasting like perfume. And this drink is refreshing enough to cool you down on the hottest days, something we're familiar with after years of baking through New York City summers! When entertaining, Elisa likes to serve this lemonade in vintage Champagne flutes and with rose ice cubes (see Tip).

1½ cups (*300 g*) sugar

1½ cups (*360 ml*) strained fresh lemon juice (from 9 to 11 lemons), plus 1 lemon, thinly sliced, for garnish

¼ cup (*60 ml*) elderflower syrup or elderflower liqueur

1½ teaspoons rose water

Ice

Miniature edible rosebuds, for garnish (optional)

1. In a small saucepan, combine the sugar and 1 cup (*240 ml*) water and bring to a boil, stirring to dissolve the sugar. Remove the pan from the heat and let the sugar syrup cool to room temperature.

2. In a tall glass pitcher, stir together the sugar syrup, lemon juice, elderflower syrup, and rose water. Add 7 cups (*1.7 liters*) water and stir to combine. Add a generous amount of ice and the lemon rounds.

3. Serve in tall glasses and, if desired, garnish with miniature rosebuds.

TIPS:
To make rose ice cubes, fill an ice cube tray halfway with distilled water and freeze until completely frozen, about 2 hours. Add a washed edible mini spray rose or other small edible rose to each ice cube cavity, fill to the top with distilled water, and freeze again until completely frozen, about 2 hours. The distilled water ensures the cubes will be clear, not cloudy, while the two-step freezing process keeps the roses in the middle. You can make floral ice cubes with any edible flower, including pansies, hibiscus, blue cornflowers, or lavender.

Store lemonade refrigerated in an airtight container for up to 2 days; wait to add ice and garnishes until ready to serve.

notes

....
....
....
....
....
....

HOLIDAY SANGRIA

makes 6-8 drinks

....

Whether for a party at home or one of our many holiday season events at maman, we love to serve this colorful crowd-pleasing sangria. We like to say that the rosemary adds some je ne sais quoi, but its real advantage is that it cuts the sangria's sweetness and creates a more balanced and complex flavor. Good wine makes good sangria, so don't cheap out on the wine! And here's a tip: If you freeze the whole cranberries, they can double as ice. For a more festive garnish, roll damp rosemary sprigs in granulated sugar.

½ cup (*60 g*) cranberries

1 (*750 ml*) bottle good white wine, such as Pinot Grigio or Chardonnay

1 cup (*240 ml*) sparkling apple cider

2 tablespoons simple syrup (see Tip)

1 Granny Smith apple (about 5 ounces / *140 g*), cut into ½-inch (*1.25 cm*) cubes

10 to 12 fresh rosemary sprigs

1. Cut ¼ cup (*30 g*) of the cranberries in half.

2. In a large pitcher, combine the white wine, sparkling apple cider, simple syrup, apple, 4 sprigs of the rosemary, and the whole and halved cranberries. Slowly stir to combine. Cover and refrigerate for at least 4 hours or overnight.

3. Serve chilled, with some of the fruit in each glass and garnished with the remaining rosemary sprigs.

TIP: *To make simple syrup, bring equal parts sugar and water to a boil over high heat, stirring to dissolve the sugar. You need only 2 tablespoons here, but it's difficult to make such a small amount, and simple syrup will keep refrigerated in an airtight container for a few weeks—use it to sweeten cocktails, tea, and other drinks.*

notes

HORTENSE'S PINK MIMOSA

makes 6-8 drinks

....

This twist on a classic mimosa honors Hortense, our former events director and a
forever member of the maman family. Hortense loves all things pink and always drinks
Champagne, so grapefruit juice with rosé bubbles is a perfect way to celebrate her. At
home, we serve this pale pink drink in Ben's maman's vintage Champagne coupe glasses.
To add even more color, we garnish with berries and sometimes edible rose petals.

1 (*750 ml*) bottle rosé
Champagne, chilled

2 cups (*480 ml*) strained fresh
pink grapefruit juice (from about
3 grapefruit), chilled, plus
1 grapefruit, sliced, for garnish

Raspberries, for garnish (optional)

Fill six to eight Champagne flutes or coupe glasses
halfway with rosé Champagne (see Tip), then top
with pink grapefruit juice. Garnish with grapefruit
slices and raspberries (if using) and serve.

TIP: *Pouring Champagne (or any bubbly beverage)
at an angle helps to minimize the foam in the glass.*

PEACH-THYME BELLINIS

makes 6 drinks

....

Come summer, Elisa always hits the local farmers' market to fill her basket with fresh peaches—and this thyme-infused cocktail is just the thing to make the fragrant stone fruit shine. Bellinis are Italian, but they're part of the French aperitif repertoire and a staple at our brunches, both at home and at maman. They pair perfectly with Croissant Pain Perdu (page 34) for a light brunch. This refreshing puree can also be added to soda water, lemonade, or iced tea.

2 cups (*85 g*) diced peeled peaches (about 6 peaches)

⅓ cup (*75 ml*) honey

1 tablespoon fresh thyme leaves, plus 6 fresh thyme sprigs for garnish

1 (*750 ml*) bottle Champagne, chilled

TIP: *Store in an airtight container for up to 7 days.*

1. In a medium saucepan, bring the peaches, honey, thyme leaves, and ½ cup (*120 ml*) water to a boil over high heat. Reduce the heat to medium and boil until the peaches are soft and falling apart and the mixture has a puree-like consistency, 8 to 10 minutes. Remove the pan from the heat and let cool slightly.

2. Transfer the cooled peach mixture to a food processor or blender and puree until completely smooth with no chunks, about 1 minute. Cover and refrigerate for at least 1 hour.

3. Fill six Champagne flutes or coupe glasses halfway with the peach puree, then top with Champagne, garnish with thyme sprigs, and serve.

notes

ANDREA'S GREEN BLOODY MARY

makes 6-8 drinks

Our marketing director, Andrea, a recent Bloody Mary convert, created this fun green twist on the classic recipe. Bloody Marys are always a hit at brunch, and using a homemade mix ensures your drinks will be fresh and free from preservatives and artificial ingredients—it also means you can customize the recipe to suit your palate. With tomatillos, yellow tomatoes, green apple, cucumber, poblano, and jalapeño, this vivid concoction is bright and refreshing. We think it has the perfect level of kick, but you can adjust the peppers, hot sauce, and horseradish to tame the heat or punch it up.

9 tomatillos (about 1 pound 6 ounces / *620 g*), husked and chopped

2 yellow tomatoes (about 9 ounces / *252 g*), diced

½ green apple (about 3 ounces / *84 g*), peeled and chopped

½ medium cucumber (about 5 ounces / *140 g*), peeled and chopped

1 poblano pepper (about 4 ounces / *113 g*), seeds removed and flesh chopped

1 tablespoon chopped seeded jalapeño

1 garlic clove, peeled

2 tablespoons prepared horseradish, plus more to taste

5 teaspoons Worcestershire sauce

1 tablespoon dill pickle juice

1 teaspoon green hot sauce

Dash of paprika

Fine sea salt and freshly ground black pepper

Lime wedges, for rimming the glass and for garnish

Celery stalks, mini dill pickles, and green olives, for garnish

Ice

9 to 12 ounces (*265 to 355 ml*) vodka

1. In a blender, combine the tomatillos, tomatoes, apple, cucumber, poblano, jalapeño, and garlic and blend on medium-high for about 1 minute to liquefy. Add the horseradish, Worcestershire sauce, pickle juice, hot sauce, and paprika and blend until fully combined. Season to taste with salt and black pepper.

2. Spread fine sea salt on a small plate. Run a lime wedge along the rim of six to eight highball glasses, then dip the top of each glass in the salt to create a thin sea salt rim.

3. Cut the celery according to the height of your glasses, leaving some of the leafy greens still attached. Skewer the mini dill pickles and green olives on toothpicks (see Tip).

4. Add ice to the highball glasses, then divide the Bloody Mary mixture evenly among the glasses. Add 1½ ounces (*44 ml*) vodka to each glass and stir to incorporate. Garnish with lime wedges, celery, and the olive and pickle skewers. Serve immediately.

TIP: *For a fun interactive brunch, set up a DIY Bloody Mary bar so your guests can pick out and skewer their own custom mix of garnishes.*

merci

"The best kinds of people are the ones that come into your life and make you see the sun when you once saw clouds, the people who believe in you so much that you start to believe in you, too, and the people who love you for being you."

—UNKNOWN

So many people have come together to make the dream of maman and this book a reality for us, and for that we extend our deepest merci beaucoup.

To our families . . .
Our sincerest gratitude goes to our families, especially our parents, for filling our childhood tables with so many wonderful memories and for raising us in homes filled with so much love, laughter, and good food. You are the true inspiration behind maman and the reason for our love of the kitchen. Thank you for always being so supportive and for encouraging our crazy dreams. From helping us pack for our next move across the ocean to being on your hands and knees to sand vintage chairs before opening each new location, we could never have accomplished what we have without your guidance, passion, and support.

To our customers . . .
For allowing maman to be an extension of your home, for making us your daily stop before work and go-to lunch spot, and for gathering your friends and family to celebrate with us. Your continued support, loyalty, kind comments, and sweet enthusiasm inspire us to keep creating, cooking, baking, and brewing. You are the real reason for our success, and we are humbled and honored to be part of your lives.

To our staff . . .
Present, past, and future—you make our days easier, and each one of you has been an integral part of our success over the past few years. A special thank-you to those who graciously shared and trusted us with your cherished family recipes and memories. We would not be where we

are today without you, and we definitely couldn't have taken the time away from the restaurant to write this book, so for that we are eternally grateful.

To Leigh . . .
A heartfelt thank-you to the best literary agent one could wish for. Your knowledge, support, and amazingly detailed recaps have helped us bring this vision to life, and it is because of your unwavering confidence in us and expertise in the industry that you now hold this book in your hands.

To Lauren . . .
For understanding us and this book so perfectly, and whose taste and advice we can always trust. Thank you for your endless patience, for putting up with our poor spelling and grammar, for your enthusiasm, and for all your hard work. Your attention to detail, insight, and gentle nudges have made this book and each recipe so special.

To Andrea . . .
Our appreciation to you is greater than words could ever express. You have been our right hand, our jack-of-all-trades, and our biggest cheerleader. Thank you for making work more fun and a great deal calmer, and for making our lives a little more beautiful with all that you do. You always surpass our expectations with your dedication, creativity, and resourcefulness. We are so lucky to have you in our lives.

To Tawni, Jean-Louis, Caitlin, Vanessa, and Kristin . . .
Thank you for sharing your words, your craft, your family recipes, and your tremendous talents with us. Each of you created, tested, and retested so many of

our delicious recipes, and we are forever thankful for your palates, culinary knowledge, and passion for the kitchen.

To the Clarkson Potter team . . .

Thank you to the entire team of brilliant individuals at Clarkson Potter. To Amanda Englander, for seeing a book in our café and helping us put to paper what maman is all about. To Raquel Pelzel, for stepping in and seeing us through the journey to creating the book we've always dreamed of writing. It's been a joy to work with all of you, including Marysarah Quinn, Heather Williamson, Kristen Casemore, and Stephanie Davis. We are so thankful for this opportunity to share so many wonderful memories from our kitchens.

To Rachel, Brooke, and the Krupa family . . .

Thank you for taking a chance on maman when it was just a concept. We would never be where we are today without you. Thank you for supporting us, encouraging us, and being our biggest champions. You not only helped get maman on the map—and on Oprah's map—but also believed in us every step of the way, and for that we are incredibly grateful. We are so happy to have had you as part of the maman family, our personal family, and story. You make our jobs and lives easier and we love you so much!

To Linda, Monica, and Kate . . .

Thank you for lending your incredible talents to our book. We could not be happier with how you captured maman's food, drinks, and vibe and helped us make the perfectly imperfect muted mess. You made us and our food look beautiful, and we feel beyond blessed to have collaborated with you all on this book.

To Leatal . . .

Like you always do, you brought an abundance of beauty to our "office" and kitchen and helped make our long photo-shoot days more enjoyable. Your florals were the perfect finishing touch to every photo, and we love having you and your work part of our book.

To Karen and Candice . . .

My most creative friends! Thank you for sharing your talents and artistry. Karen, you created a font that reminds me of my maman's handwriting and added so much beauty and warmth to our cookbook, not to mention our menus, our windows, and every sign we ever make. Candice, your patterns make everyone's morning coffee a little more beautiful and our cups such a sought after fashion accessory! Because of you, I can say I have the prettiest garbage in NYC!

To Brett . . .

Thank you for listening to our dreams over many glasses of wine, for believing in us and our concept, and for all your continued support. You were such a key part of creating maman and turning those dreams into reality, and without your trust and encouragement we would never have hit a home run and wouldn't be where we are today.

To our friends . . .

maman, our lives, and this book would not be possible if not for our dearest friends. You helped us shape this project through years of dinner parties, celebrations, and shared joys. Thank you for all your support and for always enjoying our recipe-testing leftovers.

To Crumpet . . .

And lastly, our little four-legged taste tester, who makes sure there are never any leftovers and that our floors (and counters) are always clean. Thank you for being the most excited member of the family whenever we cook and for always licking the bowl clean, even when we burn things. You are the best big brother, cuddle buddy, and companion.

Baby Yves,

The kitchen has always been the beating heart of our home and where you have spent most of your days so far, either strapped to your maman's chest or sleeping quietly through the clanking of beaters and the ringing of the smoke alarm. You have patiently sat through meetings, had naps on desks, and spent more time staring at a laptop than any child should. Maman has become a second home for you—a place where you are surrounded by your extended family, who loves you dearly and has watched you grow since the very beginning (they even put up with Mommy on no caffeine). You won't remember these early days, but we will, and we will hold them in our hearts.

It is said that the way to a man's heart is through his stomach, and just like your daddy, you have quickly taught us just how true that is. Your love (bordering on obsession) for food at such a young age inspires us and gives us hope that you might follow in our culinary footsteps. Our cooking for you is an expression of our love, a way to nourish your little body and your soul. We are looking forward to the days when you are big enough to be beside us, making a mess, licking the spoons, and hopefully cooking from this very book. We hope the greatest lessons you learn in life are around our dinner table and the greatest legacies we leave you are these beautiful family memories.

You are the truffle oil on top of our mac and cheese, the milk with our cookies, and the sweetest icing spread over our cake. You have brought us joy, laughter, comfort, and a deeper love than we could ever express in words. You have shown us the word *maman* in a whole new light, and you are by far the best thing we have ever baked.

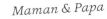

Maman & Papa

index

Note: Page references in *italics* indicate photographs.

Library of Congress Cataloging-in-Publication Data
is available upon request.

ISBN 978-0-593-13895-3
Ebook ISBN 978-0-593-13896-0

Printed in China

Photographer: Linda Xiao
Editor: Raquel Pelzel
Designer: Marysarah Quinn
Production Editor: Patricia Shaw
Production Manager: Heather Williamson
Composition: Merri Ann Morrell and Nicholas Patton
Copy Editor: Kate Slate
Indexer: Elizabeth T. Parson

10 9 8 7 6

First Edition

Elisa Marshall and **Benjamin Sormonte** are the cofounders and owners of maman. Elisa, the creative director, oversees branding, communications, and events, and works with maman's chefs to develop and fine-tune maman's recipes and menus. She's also a contributing columnist for *Martha Stewart* online. As the CEO, Ben manages operations and business development, and he is also the creative mind behind some of maman's most beloved savory dishes. Together, Elisa and Ben design the interiors of all maman locations, which can be found throughout New York City as well as in Montreal and Toronto.